Praise for The Hamster Revolution Series

A dynamic, high-impact strategy.
- Tony Robbins, Author, Unleash the Giant Within

It works!
- Ken Blanchard, Co-Author, The One Minute Manager

A fun read, but even better, a straightforward solution.
- Marcus Buckingham, author, *Now, Discover Your Strengths*

It takes guts to teach Microsoft leaders new ways to use our own technology! The Hamster Revolution exceeded expectations.
- Chuck Metzger, Sr. Program Mgr. Office 365 Team, Microsoft

A must-read business book!
- Keith Ferrazzi, author, *Never Eat Alone*

Double your productivity!
- Marshal Goldsmith, Alliant University

These practices will change the way you work. They did for us!
- Matt Koch, Dir. Of Knowledge Management, Capital One

Zip! Tips helped our busy salespeople soar!
- Brenda Davis, Worldwide Training, United Airlines

It's no stretch to say that this is life-changing material.
- Chris Granger, VP, Team Business Development, NBA

The Hamster
Revolution
for TQ

How to Thrive in the Post-Covid,
Virtual World of Work

The Hamster
Revolution
for

TECH QUOTIENT

Mike Song

Get Control! Publishing
www.getcontrol.net

for kris
forever

Personal

I dedicate this book to my family, friends, and community who helped me survive an unimaginable personal tragedy. Thank you all for raising me up and helping me find a positive path and mission for the rest of my life.

Professional

I would also like to recognize my business partner Jeff Burress who never stopped believing in TQ or me. Our twenty-year partnership has been incredibly productive and rewarding. Jeff's great ideas, energy, and passion for excellence helped bring this book to life.

CONTENTS

x

INTRODUCTION

This book is your bridge to the future of work.

We are standing at the edge of a deep, dark canyon with a river racing through it. Experts call this chasm, **The Digital Skills Gap**.

On the other side is the **Future of Work**. In that world, digital skills determine who gets hired, promoted, and fired. If you think you're immersed in Office 365 or Google Docs now, just wait. In ten years, the time you spend on technology will increase by 60%[i]. To hold your job, you'll need to master countless new apps, devices, and web tools.

Here's the scary part. Workers, organizations, and countries keep launching themselves off the ledge, falling short, and plunging into the cold, harsh waters of obsolescence.

Why do they fail? For starters, employers have no system for measuring tech proficiency. As a result, employees have no idea where they stand. Leaders are often reluctant to lead because they doubt their own digital skills. Tech-savvy colleagues exist, but no one inspires them to share the magic. As a result, attempts at **Digital Transformation** stall mid-leap – and down they go.

Sadly, Covid-19 – only made matters worse.

As the clock ticks, you find yourself stuck in the past, running in place like an exhausted hamster on a never-ending wheel of work. Without a strategic plan – how will you ever bridge the gap?

1

THE CAMELBACK CAFÉ

Our story begins in a resort hotel in Arizona just as things return to normal following a global health pandemic.

Outside the coffee shop in the lobby, a smartly dressed young woman called out in a crisp British accent, "Any chance of a tea?"

Inside, a guy who was removing chairs upended on tables motioned to his watch in the universal gesture for "Sorry, but it's not time yet."

The woman glanced at me and said apologetically. "It's terrible, isn't it? I can't survive without a splash of tea in the morning."

"I'm the same with coffee," I replied.

"Oh, well, I suppose I'll just have to wait." She turned to look out of the window. "It's certainly a stunning view."

I followed her gaze. The sun was rising over Camelback mountain.

"Now that's spectacular," I agreed.

"Too bad, I can't enjoy it."

"Why not?"

"You know, work problems. You here for business as well?"

"Yeah."

"It's a huge hotel, isn't it? And there are so many conferences going on."

"Business conferences are back with a vengeance," I joked.

"Well, I'm not looking forward to mine."

"No?"

"My company's in big trouble. We're here to sort things out."

"Sounds like serious stuff."

She pulled out her smartphone, tapped the screen, and held it out towards me.

"See that?"

The headline read: "DroneZone on Life Support!"

"Ouch," I winced. "So, what's the problem?"

"Oh, I'm not going to bore you with it all."

"Don't worry," I said. "Sometimes, it helps to talk to someone new."

She flashed me a smile. "Anyway, I'm Claire, and you are...?"

"Mike - but my friends call me Coach. So, what's up with DroneZone?"

She sighed. "I think you mean, *what's down* with DroneZone. That would be profits, productivity, and morale."

I raised my eyebrows. "Really? Why?"

"Tech challenges. Have you heard of the **Digital Skills Gap**?"

"Yeah, I've heard of that." This chat was getting more interesting by the minute.

"That's what the experts call it, but to me, it's more like the digital skills crisis. You see, to survive in this industry, you need tech-savvy employees."

"That's right."

"A lot of our people are slow to adopt new apps, devices, and digital tools. Then Covid-19 hit, and it's turned everything upside down. Suddenly, everyone's working from home and relying on technology.[ii]"

"I see."

"The thing is, we're making so many tech-related mistakes. You know, losing digital documents, using the wrong app for the job, that kind of thing."

"I understand."

"So, the competition's getting ahead of us."

"And this meeting's your last chance to turn things around?"

"That's about it. Last year, I drew the short straw. So now I'm in charge of the **Digital Transformation Task Force**. Our goal is to upskill our entire workforce. Now 10,000 colleagues, including our CEO, are anxiously awaiting a miracle that to be honest, I can't deliver."

"Drones are big now. Right? So, sales must be up."

"Are you kidding? They're way down! And that's a great example: our sales team isn't using the sales software we rolled out last year – sorry, am I boring you?"

"No, no, carry on."

"Well, instead, they're taking notes in random documents or post-its which they pop on the wall – I see them in Zoom meetings!"

"Come on; you're not serious?"

"It's true. Oh, and speaking of Zoom, we're rubbish at virtual meetings! They're dull, and people tune out, especially our clients."

"What about your leaders?"

"To be honest, they're part of the problem! They're the last ones to adopt new technology."

"Not a good situation."

"We conducted a survey, and less than 20% of our people have mastered our most basic digital tools."

"Digital tools?"

"You know, the devices and apps that *everyone* uses: Office 365, Google search, smartphones, that sort of thing. For example, when they use email, they never create rules to manage their inboxes."

"That's basic stuff."

"Spot on. The bottom line is everyone's overloaded, overwhelmed, and overworked."

"Sounds like DroneZone has 10,000 employees, all running in place like harried hamsters on 10,000 wheels!"

She thought for a moment, "You know what?"

"Go on."

"It does feel like we're spinning our wheels. And it's exhausting."

"I can imagine. So, you're here to stage a Camelback comeback?"

"That's one way of putting it. This summit may be DroneZone's last chance -" - she mimicked an ER doctor using a defibrillator - " - to revive the patient. Code blue! CLEAR!"

I laughed. I've always admired people who keep their sense of humor in difficult times.

"So, what have you tried so far?"

"Well, - Coach - two years ago, our task force asked a bunch of ivory tower gurus to show us the way. They told us to hire millennials, purchase a massive e-learning library, and convert our offices into an open floorplan."

"To boost collaboration?"

"Who knows. We also introduced a game room, sleep pods, and a *sushi bar*."

"I love sushi! Did the changes work?"

"Not one bit! And we spent a huge amount of money. And now, after COVID-19, almost everyone's working from home."

"So, lots of empty sleep pods?"

"And no queue for the sushi bar."

"Shame."

Claire shrugged, "It feels like my head is on the proverbial chopping block. And now we're bringing in another guru."

"You mean a consultant?"

"I call them vultures."

"Well, what's the next one serving up?"

"Probably another load of gibberish, I expect."

"You never know. Maybe this consultant is *the* one?"

DING-DING! Our smartwatches chimed to let us know it was finally 7 a.m. The barista appeared, flipped the café sign to open, and beckoned us to enter.

"Finally," Claire said. "Caffeine!"
"Our long-lost friend," I said. "I'm a mochaccino kind of guy."

"I'm an Earl Grey gal."

"Very English."

"Definitely - an English hamster, you might say."

After we paid for our drinks, Claire glanced at her watch and let out a gasp. "Oh, my Gosh! Is that the time? I have to run."

"Nice meeting you," I said.

"Yeah, same here. And thanks for listening."

As I watched her hurry off, I took a big sip of coffee and thought, *This is going to be interesting.*

2

A DAY IN THE LIFE

Harold, the COO at DroneZone, and an old friend greeted me with a broad smile when I arrived at the conference room entrance on the second floor.

"Hey, Coach! Good to see you again," he said warmly.

"Hi, Harold, it's been a long time."

"Everyone's excited to hear you speak."

But maybe not Claire, I thought.

"I'll need you to wait in the hall for a few minutes while our CEO Maria Zampa covers a few things."

"I saw her on *Business Update* a couple of years ago. As I recall, she was quite impressive."

"That year, she made the Forbes' Top 100 Innovative Leaders List."

"Wow!"

"Listen, your PC's plugged in, and the cover slide is up on the big screen."

"Great! Then I'm ready to roll."

"I'll send our new intern, Tameeka, out to get you."

He ducked back into the room, and through the door, I glimpsed Claire deep in conversation with another executive. *This will be fun,* I thought to myself.

It wasn't long before a cheerful young woman stuck her head out of the door.

"Hi! They're ready for you now."

"Thanks, Tameeka!"

As I entered the room, Claire did a double-take.

"Well, this takes the biscuit," she said in a low voice as I passed her.

I grinned and gestured *Hi again!*

Harold was standing at the front of the room beside a table, which, I was pleased to see, contained two bottles of water and a glass. In front of him sat about twenty execs, spread out over five tables with their laptops open. After introducing me to Maria, he cleared his throat and addressed the room. "OK, folks, as you know, DroneZone is suffering from a digital skills midlife crisis. All our attempts at upskilling our workforce have come up short. And that's why I've invited Mike - well, everyone calls him Coach - to our meeting. He's a tech turnaround expert. I met him through my last job, at Foster and Schrubb, and his ideas are, well, revolutionary."

Harold turned to me and said, "You've got thirty minutes, Coach."

"Thanks, Harold. Good morning, everyone! There's not much time, so I'm going to jump straight in. I've conducted over 100,000 surveys that examine the real world in which people work. So, let's see if I can describe a typical day-in-the-life for your average employee. It helps if I can use a real person's name."

"How about Dita from Sales," said Claire, pointing at a small woman in a beige pantsuit.

"Hey," said Dita. "Why's everyone always picking on Sales?"

"They shouldn't," said Maria. "Without you, we're all out of a job."

"Thank you for playing along, Dita," I said, and then in an announcer's voice, added, "A Day in the Life of a DroneZone Colleague - take one! Dita wakes up and starts her morning ritual. Almost every day, she has an unexpected personal challenge. Maybe she can't find her daughter's backpack - or the cat threw up on the sofa."

Dita smiled. "And sometimes the cat throws up on the backpack!"

"Yikes! She resolves these problems and gets to work. She opens her PC and finds a mountain of emails and chats. Slowly, she begins to process them, but at 10:13 a.m., a surprise task pops into her life. Maybe it's an urgent text from a big client or an important email from a colleague. Suddenly, Dita's plan for a productive day starts to veer off course."

"Ouch," said an exec sitting at the back.

I paused. "Sound familiar?"

The executives issued a chorus of groans and nods. I was hitting the mark.

"At 10:45, Dita struggles to find an important PDF related to that surprise task. She loses track of time and arrives five minutes late to her 11 a.m. web meeting."

"That's early for us!" said another exec.

"She's on DroneZone time," someone else quipped.

"OK," I continued, "the web meeting begins late. There's a tech glitch or two, an awkward introduction, and a fuzzy agenda. Dita notices that some of her people do not turn on their webcams; others have such drab lighting that they seem to be broadcasting from a cave. She wonders, *Could this be hurting our sales?* The virtual meeting - no pun intended - drones on and on. Dita gets distracted and finds herself -"

"Scrolling through cat clips on Tik Tok!" chirped Claire.

The room broke into laughter.

"OK! Well, after her social media binge, Dita winds down the day in a losing battle with her ever-expanding task list. She works on projects, struggles to complete action items, and fields texts on her phone. She feels like she's getting nowhere fast, like an exhausted hamster running on a perpetual wheel at work."

I glanced at Claire, and she smiled back.

"Raise your hand if this sounds like a typical day at Dronezone," I said.

One by one, almost all the execs raised their hands.

"Have you been reading my diary?" asked Dita.
The group chuckled nervously.

Maria said, "It's not so funny. We're spinning our wheels while our competition is pulling away."

The comment hung in the air.

"Funny you should say that, Maria," I said.
I advanced my slide to reveal a cartoon of an exhausted looking businessman running on a hamster wheel. Soft music began playing in the background.

"Your people are spinning their wheels at work, like 10,000 exhausted hamsters on 10,000 hamster wheels. Round and round they go, day after day after day."

My voice and the music grew louder. The executives seemed both amused and bewildered.

"I know things look grim. DroneZone's on life support. And we all know that the digital skills crisis is only getting worse. Well, I say, enough! It's time to fight back. It's time to try something bold and new. Drastic times call for drastic measures."

"Yes, but can you please get to the point?" said Claire.

"I've got a plan that transforms hamsters into energetic, productive employees who – get this – love their jobs. They love those jobs because when you get more done, you have more fun."

I cut the music and paused for effect.

"It's time for – the Hamster Revolution!"

3

Z IS FOR ZIP

A few of the execs looked puzzled at my announcement.

I paused for a bit as several hotel staff quietly entered the room and placed cookies, coffee, and tea at the back.

Finally, Claire broke the suspense. "OK," she said, "what exactly is the Hamster Revolution?"

"A strategic plan for achieving digital transformation. Before I walk you through the plan, I need you all to commit to one thing."

"Which is?" said Maria.

"Zip."

"Come again?"

"We must pack the initiative with zip tips."

"What on earth are zip tips?" asked Claire.

"Zip tips are tech tips that make people say, *"Wow! That's useful! Tell me more."*

Several of the executives shifted uncomfortably in their seats.

"Go on," said Maria.

"Well, if you want to create a wave of digital change at DroneZone, you need to make people say, *Wow!*"

I walked to the back of the room and slowly turned around. "And that is my favorite thing to do."

"Why are zip tips so important?" asked Maria.

"Most attempts to transform a workforce fail because there's no way to sustain interest and energy. People tune out. They return to their old habits. But a regular dose of zip delivers that *Wow!* moment that re-engages everyone."

"Like a buzzworthy post on social media," suggested Tameeka.

I gestured towards Tameeka. "She gets it. No zip, no buzz. No buzz, no change."

Maria looked skeptical. "Mm. Can you show us a zip tip?"

"Yes," said Dita. "After that awful day in my life, it's the least you could do."

Advanced Email Search

"OK, I'll make this quick. Everyone, please nod if you've searched and struggled to find an email in the past twenty-four hours."

All heads bobbed in agreement.

"Let's zip to a better way to complete that task. Here's my Outlook inbox? I believe that's what you use?"

Harold nodded in recognition.

"OK! *Urgent Scenario:* I need to find a critical message from last month with an important attachment, sent by my boss, Jeff Brown. What do I do?"

"Type Jeff Brown and some keywords, I suppose," shrugged Claire.

"There's a much better way."

I clicked my email search window.

"First, I'll do it your way – I'll use keywords. But let's break it down into steps. I·type Jeff's last name and hit *Enter*. See? Bad news. Most of the results:

- Are not from Jeff
- Do not have an attachment and
- Are not from last month.

"So what?" said Claire. "Just keep typing keywords."

"But I do that all day long," said Dita wearily.

"Here's a new way. This time, I click in the search box and notice that a new search ribbon has appeared."

Z is for Zip

The execs looked surprised as they studied the screen.

"This time, I click the *From* button, I type *Brown* and hit *Enter*. See? Instantly, my inbox displays only emails from Jeff Brown, highlighted in yellow."

Maria arched her eyebrows. "Do any of us do that?" she asked, looking around.

Most of her team shook their heads.

"Now," I continued, "let's click on **Has Attachments** and **Last Month** and…Boom! With just two clicks, I've instantly narrowed the results to three messages."

I heard quiet gasps in the room.

"You see? I zipped to that message in just three extra clicks. And guess what? You can do the same thing with Gmail."

"I'll be using Gmail during my senior year," said Tameeka.

"We use it at home," said Harold.

"Just look for a downward pointing arrow on the right side of the Gmail search window," I said, quickly opening my Gmail account and circling it with my red laser pointer.

"See?"

"I've never seen that Outlook search ribbon," said Dita, looking bemused. "How long has it been there?"

"Over ten years."

"Coach taught me this zip tip at Foster and Schrubb," said Harold. "I showed it to my team – and now everyone uses it."

"That's twice as fast as my typical search," said Maria.

I said, "Raise your hand if that was a *Wow!* moment for you."

Hands shot up, and I felt a familiar, warm sensation in my chest. I'd always gotten a kick out of helping people zip.

"If I'm lucky enough to work with DroneZone," I said. "I have to insist that we build plenty of zips into the program.

Agreed?"

"I'm all for that," said Maria. "What's next?"

Need more tech tips from Coach?
*Text **tqtips** to **22828***
and get a zip each month!

4

IQ, EQ, AND TQ

"OK, Coach," said Harold, "why don't you walk us through your Hamster plan."

Before I could speak, the door swung open, and a stern-looking, red-faced guy strode in and plopped himself down in the back row."

"Nice of you to join us, Cal," said Claire sarcastically.

"Yeah, sorry, my meeting with GCC ran late." He motioned towards me. "Another talking head?"

Claire introduced me to Cal and explained that he was DroneZone's Chief Financial Officer - the guy who controlled the budget.

"Carry on," said Claire as she signaled to me to continue.

"Zip tips alone won't get DroneZone's hamsters off their wheels. You need a strategic plan that changes the fundamental way your people think about technology."

"Zip tips? Hamsters?" said Cal, "What's this all about?"

"The Coach was about to show us his approach to digital transformation. He calls it The Hamster Revolution," explained Maria, and then gave Cal a summary of what I'd said previously.

"Alright," he said cautiously. "But didn't we just spend good money on the last tech expert's foolproof plan?"

"Tell me about that project, Cal," I said, taking a sip of water.

He began counting on his fingers, "We offered IT training, pop-up tech sessions, lunch and learns, videos, webinars - you name it."

"Cal's right," said Harold, "it was a lot of work."

"How'd it go?"

"Not so well," said Cal. "Right, Claire?"

She puffed out her cheeks. "Low attendance, low ratings, and no visible signs of progress. As Chief Learning Officer, I get to own that disaster - forever."

"Listen," said Maria, holding up her hand, "if anyone's responsible for this setback, it's all of us, especially me."

Claire looked relieved. I felt a lump in my throat. I've always loved leaders who own setbacks and share victories.

"Maybe our people just need a kick in the butt?" suggested Cal.

"So, what's the plan?" asked Maria.

IQ, EQ, and TQ

"The Hamster Revolution is a one-month digital transformation project. The goal is to increase tech proficiency by 30% across the entire organization."

Cal rolled his eyes. "Promises, promises."

"Listen, I can understand your skepticism, but trust me. If we do it right, your organization will see a 10% increase in productivity as well as a time savings of more than ten days a year."
"Per person?" asked Dita.

"Yes. That's about 20 minutes a day."

"Yeah, but how is this different from the last project?" said Cal.

"TQ," I replied.

"I'm afraid to ask, but what is TQ?" said Maria.

"It stands for Technology Quotient. It's a new way to measure tech proficiency."

Now it was Claire's turn to look skeptical. "How on earth can you measure that?"

"I suppose you'll need a revolutionary new assessment tool," I said.

"We will?"

"Sure. I'll bet you measure all kinds of skills at DroneZone. Why not measure tech skills too?"

"This seems sketchy," said Cal.

I advanced to my next slide.

"Now, I'll bet you measure IQ to find the best and brightest people. Right?"

"Of course," said Claire.

"I'll also wager you assess EQ, that's Emotional Intelligence, to find and develop people who work well with others. Right?
"All of our managers take the Emotional and Social Competence Inventory (ESCI) assessment."

"With great results, I might add," said Maria.

"So, you measure IQ and EQ – that's great. But your people spend all day immersed in *technology*. Why not measure TQ?

The room fell silent.

"I wouldn't know where to begin," said Claire.

"I'm not sure it's possible," said Cal. "I mean, every division uses different software apps."

"True," I said, "but there is common ground. Almost everyone at DroneZone uses 365, browsers, and Google search. Right?"

"Of course," said Harold, looking intrigued. "We spend half the day on Outlook and Teams."

Dita held up her phone. "And smartphones too."

"We've built an assessment that measures how well all of your people use these universal digital tools," I said. "If you're trying to transform your workforce - you need a way to measure progress across all divisions."

"So, does this tool have a name?" said Claire.

"The Tech Quotient Assessment Tool or TQAT℠ for short."

"How does the TQAT help us?" asked Maria.

"Right now, people only have a subjective understanding of their tech skills relative to others. The TQAT gives everyone a TQ score from 1-100. Once they know their score, they're motivated to improve – and we can track and reward the change."

"Ah," said Harold, "so they take the TQAT before and after training."

"This could help us find some tech rock stars," grinned Dita.

"And develop new ones," added Claire.

"Mm...We could set goals for each employee," said Maria."

I nodded. "It gets better. The TQAT can collect team, division, and organization-wide metrics. This data motivates everyone to participate and improve."

"Competition," remarked Harold. "A TQ leader board would spark the interest of every manager in the company." He motioned to the people in the room, "I wonder how we would score on this assessment."

"Interesting," said Maria. "Some of us wouldn't know a pivot table from a ping-pong table!"

Everyone laughed. An exec in the back said, "But not Cal. He's Mr. Pivot Table, our resident spreadsheet geek!"

I raised my eyebrows, "Is that true, Cal?"

"Perhaps."

"I had no idea," said Harold.

"Surprise, surprise," said Maria.

I advanced the slide to show an XY axis.

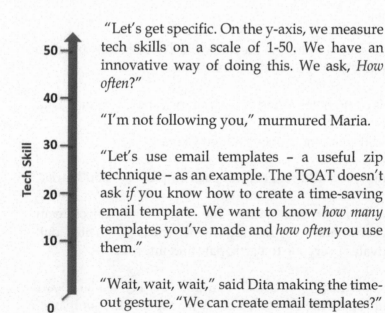

"Let's get specific. On the y-axis, we measure tech skills on a scale of 1-50. We have an innovative way of doing this. We ask, *How often?*"

"I'm not following you," murmured Maria.

"Let's use email templates – a useful zip technique – as an example. The TQAT doesn't ask *if* you know how to create a time-saving email template. We want to know *how many* templates you've made and *how often* you use them."

"Wait, wait, wait," said Dita making the time-out gesture, "We can create email templates?"

"Sure," I said, "Take a look."
I showed the execs how to create and insert Outlook email

and Gmail templates. The executives spent five minutes brainstorming all the ways that templates could save time while improving communication.

Harold said, " Now I see why you ask *how many* templates we use. The more we use a best practice, the more productive we become."

Cal smirked, "So everyone's going to lie and say, *I have a hundred templates!* The results will be meaningless."

"Well," I replied, "most people are honest. But the TQAT rewards improvement over baseline. We let them know it's harder to improve upon an artificially high score. Focusing on the pre to post results encourages people to be truthful."

"IQ + EQ + TQ," said Maria. "I must say, that sounds like a pretty good formula for career success."

"Yet, we only measure IQ and EQ," said Harold, thoughtfully. "And, given our digital skills crisis, that suddenly seems odd."

"Bingo," I said with a smile, "And once you've helped the entire organization boost TQ with their basic digital tools, that newfound proficiency can be directed at job-specific apps like that sales software Dita mentioned."

Harold wandered to the back of the room and picked up a cookie. Turning to the group, he said, "The Hamster Revolution has evolved since my days at Foster and Schrubb."

"Thanks, Harold," I said. "Maybe we should all grab a cookie and stretch our legs?"

"Hold on," said Cal. "You said the total score was 100. But the tech score only goes up to 50 points."

I nodded. "Uh-huh."
"Well, what about the other 50?"

"That's the best part," I said. "Get ready for **The Power of X.**"

Zip Tip: Email Templates

Outlook Email Templates
- Open an Outlook email
- On the far-right ribbon Click *View Templates*
- At the bottom of the panel that opens on the right, click the *plus-circle Template* button and add your text
- To use, place your mouse in the body of the email and double click the preferred template

Gmail Email Templates
- Open an email and create the template text
- In the lower-right corner, click the *three-dot button*
- Click *Save draft as template* > *Save as new template*
- Name and click *Save*
- To use, place the cursor in the body of email > Click the same *three-dot button* > Click the preferred template

5

THE POWER OF X

I took a mouthwatering bite of chewy, double chocolate peanut butter cookie and walked to the front of the room. One-by-one, the execs took their seats. Harold stayed in the back, as I'd instructed.

"Ready? I asked, suddenly raising my arms in a dramatic gesture. "Behold!"

Boom! A loud clap of thunder startled everyone. The lights went out, and ominous music filled the air.

An unnaturally deep robotic voice said, "The information you are about to receive is top-secret, classified, and proprietary. The X-Factor represents a breakthrough in digital transformation technology."

The execs laughed at my theatrics as a giant X slowly emerged on the screen.

"OK, Harold," I said. "You can hit the lights and grab a seat."

"Sorry if we startled you," said Harold, flicking the lights back on. "The coach put me up to this on the cookie break."

"This is nuts," said Cal.

"OK, Coach," said Claire. "So, what's this X-Factor stuff all about?"

"I'm trying to make a point. The Power of X is a big deal. It's the second component of the TQ score." I advanced the slide to show a full XY chart. "Of course, I'm talking about the horizontal x-axis on the TQ chart."

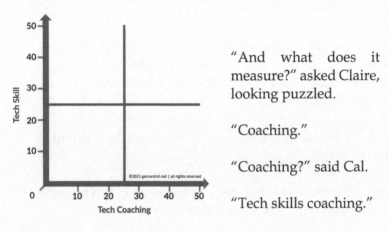

"And what does it measure?" asked Claire, looking puzzled.

"Coaching."

"Coaching?" said Cal.

"Tech skills coaching."

"Hmm, this chart reminds me of something," said Maria.

"Tech coaching is the ability to share useful tech ideas."

"Ah," said Maria brightly.

"Your mission is a tough one. You're trying to upskill the entire workforce."

"We know that," said Cal dismissively.

"Moving a mountain takes teamwork and leadership. In addition to great training, you need enthusiastic coaches and cheerleaders to spread the word. I'm not always right, Cal. But I'm sure about this: X marks the spot when it comes to these big rollouts."

"Coaching seems like a tough skill to develop," observed Claire.

"You'd be surprised. All it takes is a little push."

"From whom?" challenged Cal.

I waved my hand across the room. "From leaders like you."

Maria looked up. "I'm not sure we have time for that."

"Understood. Perhaps, I can take you through an accelerated program to get you up to speed. But Maria..." I paused to consider my words. "There is a right way and a wrong way to do this. And in my honest opinion –"

"I get it," she said, holding up her hand, "You need us to walk the walk, or no one will take it seriously."

"And I promise to make it useful and fun," I said.

"Can you give me an example of an X-Factor question?" she said, "I'm having trouble seeing how you sort these people out of the crowd."

"Here's an example; *How often do you share useful smartphone tips with your entire team?*"

"I see how that might work," said Claire tentatively.
"To be honest, it was challenging to develop these questions. And even harder to perfect an algorithm."

"But it looks like you did it," said Dita, "Can you describe a person with high X and Y scores?"

"There are no absolutes. But I find they're usually successful, leaders who are well-liked by colleagues. They get a kick out of delivering *Wow!* moments."

"We certainly need more people like that," noted Maria.

"They're rare," I said. "The program you rolled out struggled because it lacked a healthy dose of Vitamin X."

"Seriously?" said Cal, "Another X slogan?"

"X-actly," I said with a grin.

"Hmm," said Claire glancing out the window at the mountains in the distance. "So, this could help us find coaches to power-up the next rollout."

"A well-executed TQ Initiative needs people who like to talk about TQ. They get everyone buzzing."

"In sales, "said Dita, "We call that word of mouth."

I nodded and pointed to my screen.

"And now we can rank your people from first to worst. When you highlight your top 10 employees on a leaderboard, everyone gets into the game."

"So, TQ coaches," said Harold, "like sports coaches, can help people improve and see them win in a real competition. That's a game-changer."

The Power of X

I opened my arms wide to the room. "It's a timeless strategy. We compete in sports, music, sales, and academics; why not TQ?"
I could see the idea taking root in the room.

"Let's take a closer look at the scoring," I said, " As you can see, the x and y scores both range from 0-50."

"So, a perfect score is 100," said Cal. I could tell he was a very completive guy.

"You bet."

"And the X Factor buzz," mused Claire, " addresses L&D's biggest challenge: attendance."

Tameeka giggled, and the room turned to see what was so funny.

"Kardashians."

"Excuse me?" said Maria.

"This is just like social media and reality TV. The hamster program creates influencers, TQ Influencers – just like on Insta or Tik Tok!"
This time, I was the one caught off guard.

"I, I never thought of it that way, Tameeka. But yeah, adding the X-Factor helps TQ go viral, like a trending topic on social media."

Maria laughed. "TQ Kardashians! Now I've heard everything."

"Oh, brother!" said Cal, shaking his head.

I held up my hand, "I've saved the best for last. The TQAT answers the single most critical question of all: ***What's your tech type?***

Want more tech tips from Coach?
Sign up for his blog!
https://www.getcontrol.net/blog

6

WHAT'S YOUR TECH TYPE?

"My tech type?" said Claire. "I have no idea."

I advanced the slide to show four professionals standing side by side.

"Have you ever wondered why some people embrace technology while others run from it?"

"All the time," said Dita. "Some of my salespeople use the new CRM while others won't touch it with a ten-foot pole."

I covered my eyes and peeked through my fingers. "Dita, please don't tell me they're taking notes on paper."

Dita's face lit up. "They are. And it drives me nuts."

Claire, who had explained this bad habit to me earlier, rolled her eyes and said, "It's like you're a mind reader, Coach."

"Isn't it crazy?" I said with a grin, "Surely, we all agree that different people relate to technology in different ways. Yet, most leaders fail to consider this fact when trying to boost tech proficiency."

Harold said, "I see what you're saying. We've been taking a one-size-fits-all approach, with poor results."

"Speaking of tech types," said Maria, "why don't more of us like to share what we know about technology?"
"There are many reasons. Managers rarely praise direct reports for sharing tech tips with the team. As a result, colleagues keep zip tips to themselves, like grain locked in a silo. We call this hoarding behavior **The Silo Syndrome**."

"Interesting," said Claire. "There's little incentive to share tech know-how."

"Right. And many other factors contribute to The Silo Syndrome."

- Busy: *I've got no time to help others!*
- Introversion: *I'm shy!*
- False Assumptions: *Oh, everybody knows that tip!*
- Hoarding: *Why give away my competitive advantage?*
- Fear: *My boss told me to get back to work.*

"Oh, that last one is awful," said Maria, pulling a face.

"And all too common. When a leader is behind the curve with technology, they may feel insecure. To them, it seems like their direct reports are showing them up."

"But work is technology," said Dita.

"And technology is work," chuckled Harold. "Maybe tech sharing should be a stated DroneZone value?"

"And added to job descriptions and performance reviews," suggested Maria.

"I agree. And terms like nerd or geek position tech coaches as oddballs. A synonym for geek is freak."

A few people looked in the direction of Cal, who moments earlier had been called "the spreadsheet geek."

"Using those words isn't a crime," I said, "but we should be firing up our tech stars and encouraging them to share."

I wandered back to where Cal was sitting.

"Cal's not a geek. He's an Excel power user. This guy is probably moving 20% faster than everyone else. His hard-won knowledge could help us all."

"You can call me a geek; just give me a 20% raise," said Cal, smiling at Maria.

"So cut to the chase," said Claire, "What are these different tech types?"

"We've uncovered four unique Tech Quotient Profiles℠ or -."

"Let me guess," giggled Claire, "TQPs for short?"

"You got me," I said, lifting my arms in mock surrender. "I'm guilty of acronym soup. The challenge is that we're breaking new ground. Some of these concepts, like tech type, have never had a name. So, please don't hate me for sharing two more TQ terms with you.

The Technosphere is the entire array of devices, websites, and apps available to a professional. The digital tools they pluck from Technosphere and begin to use make up their

Digital Office. The organization and optimization of each employee's digital office is a critical TQ goal."

"How might I optimize my digital office?" asked Claire. "Well," I said. "Everyone here at DroneZone has a 365 browser home page that offers browser versions of all the Microsoft apps."

"So what?" asked Cal. "I've got all those apps on my PC desktop."

"Actually," I said, "you don't. Some apps, like Forms, are only available in the browser format. A high TQ person would locate Forms in their technosphere, master it, and create a browser shortcut to reach it fast. That's an example of optimizing one's digital office."

"What is Microsoft Forms?" asked Harold.

"A quick and easy quiz and survey creation tool," I said.

"Can you show us?" said Maria.

I took the team on a quick tour of 365. They expressed surprise at all the browser-only apps that were available.

"That was fun," I said, "Any questions about tech types?"

"This idea seems so familiar," said Maria, "It's on the tip of my tongue."

Cal frowned. "Why does any of this matter?"

"Simple," I said. "Once we sort people into TQ Profiles, we provide targeted training, which leads to better results."

What's Your Tech Type?

"I've got it," said Maria excitedly. "Tech types remind me of *personality types* – you know, like DISC or Myers Briggs."

Harold's eyes widened. "Interesting. So, the TQAT is like the MBTI assessment, but for technology?"
I clapped my hands. "Keep going; you two are on the right path."

"I knew it," said Maria, pointing at the XY chart on the screen. "So, the TQAT sorts us into different quadrants on that chart. And each quadrant represents a unique TQ profile."

"Right! Sorting by tech type allows us to customize training and identify the best goals and roles for each participant."

I glanced around the group. "Raise your hand if you've taken a personality type assessment?"

Everyone, except Tameeka, had taken one.

"Was it useful?"

"Definitely," said Claire. "All of our managers take DISC® in phase two training. They love it. It builds self-awareness and leads to higher performing teams."

An animated discussion about personality assessments took place, with Harold explaining how all the execs at Foster and Schrubb took the MBTI® with excellent results.

As the chatter died down, I moved to the next slide to show the now-familiar TQ XY chart.

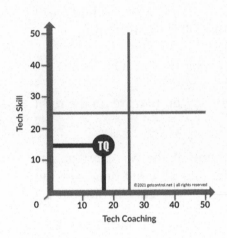

"Here's how we determine your TQP. This person scored a 15 on Tech Skill and a 17 on Tech Coaching. So, they fall into quadrant one – The Emerging Techie Profile. Each quadrant represents a different tech type."

"And their TQ is 32," mused Cal, "The sum of the two scores."

"I am gobsmacked," said Claire. "So, each of us falls into one of those quadrants?"

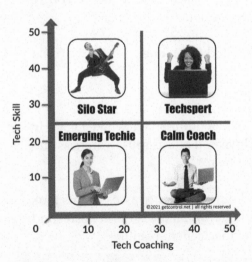

"Yes. That's exactly right."

Dita nodded. "Can you give us a quick description of each profile?"

"OK, first, in the bottom left square, we have the Emerging Techie℠. They have low tech and coaching skills. Emerging Techies make up 65% of all professionals. Technology makes them a bit nervous, but they show the most improvement during a TQ initiative."

"Lots of upside potential," remarked Harold.

What's Your Tech Type?

"Then, in the upper-left square, we have the Silo Star℠, who possesses high tech and low coaching skill."

"Selfish buggers – hoarding all the tips," said Claire.

"Next, in the bottom right quadrant, sits the Calm Coach℠. They have low tech and high-coaching skills. They're cool, calm, and collected when it comes to technology. But, for a variety of reasons, they've yet to master their everyday tech tools, like advanced Google search or Office 365."

"What kind of reasons?" asked Dita.

"Some are newer hires just out of college where they used Gmail and Google docs on a Mac. They get hired, tossed a PC, and have little time to explore their new Technosphere. Now the next profile is--"

"Drumroll, please!" said Claire. "Here comes the TQ sweepstakes winner –"

I smiled. "And, in the upper-right position, we have the Techspert℠. Just 3% of all professionals currently resides in this quadrant. But now, the organization can set a goal to increase that number to 30% or more."

"People are competitive," said Dita, "I can see how the goal of achieving Techspert status could fire them up."

"Indeed," I said, feeling the energy in the room rising. "The Techspert possesses high tech and coaching skills. They are often top performers. They constantly scan for better, smarter, and faster ways to work – and share the magic with everyone they meet."

No one said anything.

"So, what do you think? Do some of your colleagues fall into these profiles? Do you see the value of defining tech types?"

Everyone stared blankly at the screen. A little part of me wondered, *Did I lose them?*" I took a sip of coffee and stood there, expectantly.

Suddenly everyone began chatting away about TQ profiles.

"I love it," enthused Maria. "It's a logical framework for upskilling our workforce."

"The TQAT gives us a new way to measure and motivate people at the same time," said Harold, "What do you think, Tameeka?"

"As a student," said Tameeka, "this whole idea of getting better with technology has been left up to me. Now I have a plan to use when I land my first job."

"Which I hope," said Harold, "will be right here."

"Slow down, everyone," said Cal, "Before we get sucked into another costly rollout, I have some big concerns."

"OK, Cal," said Maria glancing around the room. "Does anyone else have concerns or questions about TQ?"

Several execs nodded or raised their hands.

"OK! Since time is short, let's do a quick lightning round to flesh out those objections."

What's Your Tech Type?

"Give me a sec to create a list," said Cal. He immediately began typing furiously into his PC.

"Uh oh," said Claire, "I think we're about to play Cal's favorite game!"

"Game?"

"We call it the lions' den. It's how we torture, I mean, grill consultants."

"Sounds scary, I mean, fun," I said.

"Oh, I'd be nervous if I were you," replied Claire.

Need more Zips from Coach?
*Text **tqtips** to 22828*
and get one each month!

7

INTO THE LIONS' DEN

"OK," said Maria, "let's hear everyone's concerns. Cal, do you want to go first, as usual?"

"Sure," said Cal, rising to his feet like an attorney about to grill a witness on a TV show.

"You claim to have experience at all this," he began sternly. "But you seem to be hiding a lot of details. Now, we may be hamsters, but we don't want to be your roadkill. So, show us how you've rolled this out in the past."

"Good question," I said. "We've been at this for twenty years, Cal. So, I can send you several Global 1000 case studies and white papers."

"Send them ASAP," said Cal.

"No problem. There are four phases to a TQ Initiative. Let's look at them."

TQ Initiative Rollout Schedule

1. **Baseline TQAT:** First, you take ten minutes to

complete the TQAT, and seconds later, you receive your TQ score, tech type profile overview, and action plan via email. The Action Plan directs you to the TQ video library, where you can instantly begin to boost TQ via helpful videos and e-learning.

2. **TQ Training:** Then, you attend the TQ Kick-Off Class. In most cases, this is a 90 minute or half-day webinar. We explore
   - The characteristics of your TQ profile
   - How your TQ and tech type compare to your team and
   - Helpful zip and coaching tips

3. **Post-Training Check-In Meetings:** After the big kick-off webinar, you have the option to attend two or three weekly web meetings. These 30-minute sessions reinforce and expand upon what you've learned. Each week you get a new TQ exercise to complete. In the final week, you create a one-page TQ Charter containing your plan and commitments for growing TQ in the coming year.

4. **Post-Training TQAT:** Then, after working to boost your TQ, you take the Post-TQAT to measure performance gains over baseline. We provide achievement certificates and more at this time.

The group asked a few more questions about the rollout. Then Harold said, "Can a person change tech types?"

"That's the best part," I said. "With a little work, anyone can progress to a higher TQ score and break into the next tech type level. People become motivated as they move through the process I just described."

"Terrific," said Maria. "Looks like you've answered Cal's first concern."

Smiling, I walked over to a whiteboard on the wall and wrote,

Lion 1 – Concerns 0.

"Uh, you're not the lion in this game," said Cal.

"Are you sure?" I said with a wink.

"Next concern?" said Maria.

Harold put up his hand. "Coach, this content needs to address our most significant pain points. We need to know more about the actual topics covered in the TQ training."

"Fair question, Harold. The TQAT and training focus on the three areas that will matter most in the future of work.

Focus Points for TQ Training

1. **Virtual Collaboration Skills:** We believe that running useful and engaging virtual meetings is critical because almost all communication and collaboration happen online. We focus on virtual impact and likability. We help you figure out what web meeting tool to use when and then provide specific meeting tips for Teams, Webex, Zoom, PowerPoint, and other apps.

2. **Tech-Driven Time Management:** According to the Harvard Business Review,[iii] traditional time management techniques no longer work. We need to

focus less on hard-to-use ideas like Inbox Zero and more on digital tools that help us find and complete essential tasks.

3. **Organizing Your Digital Office:** The Technosphere is rapidly expanding. Professionals are struggling to keep track of a tidal wave of new apps and digital storage sites. Whether it's OneDrive or G-Drive, people are struggling to find things fast. We help them organize, prioritize, and manage their digital world.

"We do need help in all three areas," said Claire, "Can you give us an example of a tech-driven time management zip?"

I opened my Outlook inbox and said, "One of the most significant time management fails is forgetting to complete a task sent via email. This zip turns that task into a scheduled action in a flash. All I need to do is to left-click, drag, and drop the email into the Calendar icon in the lower-left part of the screen. See? It instantly transforms itself into a calendar item with all the content of the email conveniently preserved inside.

Big smiles broke out around the room.

"Wild," said Claire, "That's new for me."

"This is the very essence of time management. I had a task; now I've scheduled time to get it done."

"Not bad," said Cal. "But what about techies who ace the TQAT? I'll bet they find this whole process to be a colossal waste of time."

I tapped the b button, and my PowerPoint presentation went black.

"I felt that way too, Cal. But I've discovered that almost everyone finds value in TQ. A few years back, a great assignment came my way. The Microsoft Office 365 Team asked me to train 80 of their top execs on – get this – the efficient use of Office 365!"

"Are you serious?" said Claire leaning forward.

"I thought, *Surely the 365 team members will know every feature of their own apps.*"

"That's what I would have thought," said Maria.

"As I began to teach the class, you could hear a pin drop. I thought, *I'm bombing!* Finally, after twenty tense minutes, one of the execs blurted out, 'This is amazing!' I could see that I had misinterpreted their silence as apathy. They even gave me a rave review on LinkedIn."

"Oh, come on," said Cal, "I can't believe that."

"I swear it's true!"

"I googled it!" said Tameeka, "It seems legit."

"Let's me see that," said Maria.

Tameeka took her laptop over to Maria.

I stood there feeling embarrassed as Maria read the review aloud.

Actual Microsoft LinkedIn Review

"It takes courage to come to Microsoft and provide shortcuts, time management, and technology benefits on our products. It is also difficult to present tech topics via the web and be successful, keep individuals' interest, and provide useable content. Mike did it all. He exceeded all expectations, delivered valuable information, and made it enjoyable, interactive, and applicable. We look forward to leveraging Mike again soon!"

Chuck Metzger, Sr. Project Manager
Microsoft Office 365 Team

"That experience showed me that TQ training could help everyone – even the techiest people on earth."

"Wow," said Harold, "Even Microsoft needs a little TQ TLC."

The group laughed. I returned to my presentation.
"What's our next concern?"

"I've got one," said Cal, looking pleased with himself.

"Go ahead. Shoot."

"We've hired a ton of young, tech-savvy employees. I'll bet our Gen Z and the Millennial hires could roll this entire initiative out on their own."

"You think so?"

"They know this stuff inside out."

"Or perhaps, it's an unproven assumption," I suggested.

Cal stood up again, "This, I have to see."

8

THE MILLENNIAL MYTH

Cal looked determined.

"So, how do you account for Millennials and Gen Z colleagues in this so-called revolution of yours? It's common knowledge that they are amazing with technology. Correct?"

I responded slowly. "Mm, I've done some research and--."

"Because," Cal added, "They grew up with it."

"We call them digital natives," noted Claire.

"And you should see them multi-task," said Dita.

"Which helps them get more done," said Cal. "I'll bet they'll be bored to death at hamster school. I think we find ten millennial or gen z mentors – and let them teach everyone else."

"Interesting," said Harold. "They now represent almost 40% of our staff."

The Millennial Myth

Claire looked thoughtful. "Millennial mentoring, that could work."

"If we cut out the middleman," said Cal, nodding in my direction, "we could save a pretty penny."

Maria said, "What say you, Coach?"

"How did you reach this conclusion?"

"It's common knowledge!" retorted Cal.

"We had a generational expert in," said Maria. "That was her main point, and she backed it up with data."

"Did she reference specific studies?" I said, "I've reviewed a few of them."

Cal typed some keywords into Google and pointed at his screen.

"I think she shared this one from Pew Research."

He abruptly unplugged my PC, projected his laptop onto the screen, and read the title,

"Millennials stand out for their technology use, but older generations also embrace digital life."

Cal pointed at the screen. "See! Pew Research says the newer generations know their stuff.[iv]"

I took a moment to scan the study.

"Folks, this study says that 93% of millennials use

smartphones vs. 90% in Gen X."

"Exactly," said Cal.

"I don't see your point, Cal. Is 3% a big difference? Isn't the real question, *How well and often do they use time-saving smartphone features?*"

Cal shook his head. "Try to keep up. You're not getting this."

I plugged my PC back into the system and projected a different study.

"Let me share some info with you. Entrepreneur Magazine, using data they commissioned from Harris Poll, came to a different conclusion. They called this article,

How the Digital Skills Gap Bleeds $1.3 Trillion a Year From US Businesses

The execs' eyes widened.

"I guess we're not alone," said Harold.

"That title validates this task force," said Maria firmly.

"Let me scroll down and show you what they discovered about Gen Z and the Millennials. Here it is, 'only 14 percent of those between 18 and 34 years old consider themselves experts[v]' when it comes to essential digital tools like Excel."

"14%?" said Maria.

I sensed the rest of the group was unsettled. I knew what I was about to say would make them even more uncomfortable.

"I believe that most of the negative assumptions made about these younger generations are way off. I think they're bright, entrepreneurial, and incredibly responsible."

"I sense a *But* coming," said Tameeka.

"I may be wrong, but I think the idea that they're light years ahead of other generations when it comes to digital skills is a myth. I call it, The Millennial Myth."

"And this is what you've seen at other organizations?" said Claire.

"Yes. In analyzing TQAT results, I've had a chance to test our generational assumptions. I've found that we overvalue youth and undervalue experience when guessing who has high TQ."

"Maybe we aren't such dinosaurs after all," said Dita.

"Far from it," I said.

"Well, that's ironic," said Claire, "because we try to avoid stereotypes, but we walked right into this one."

"I wonder if we've shortchanged these newer generations," said Maria.

"Er, what do you mean?" asked Cal.

"By assuming they know everything, we've missed a chance to help them grow."

"Good point. Remember, TQ is all about best practices," I said. "The TQAT asks precise questions. For example, *Do you use meeting templates to save time? If so, how many?*"

"What have you found?" asked Harold.

"In my experience, Millennials use meeting templates at the same rate as everyone else."

"I hate to keep asking, but about those templates, said Dita. "Can you show us how you use them?"

"Nope," I said with a smile, "Because you can use the same 365 template tool I showed you earlier for meetings. In Google Calendar, you can create a dummy calendar invite, find it by search, make a copy, and use it again and again."

"Thanks!"

"I still think you're missing the point," said Cal, undaunted.

I thought for a minute. Then, I had an idea.

"Let's do a quick thought experiment to prove my point. **Scenario:** We're all on a spaceship that's about to crash into some planet."

"Which planet?" called out someone at the back.

"You choose," I said.

"Uranus!" he yelled.

Everyone snickered at once, including me.

The Millennial Myth

"This meeting is unraveling," said Cal.

"OK, to avoid crashing into Uranus, either Cal or Tameeka has to do some quick Excel calculations. Your job is to choose the best person to crunch the numbers. Think fast; lives are at stake. Will it be Tameeka or Cal?"

"Gen Z vs. Gen X," said Dita.

"Hey!" cried Tameeka, "I'm just an intern – and I use Google Sheets at school, not Excel."

"But you're from Gen Z," I said. "I'm sure you'll figure it out."

Another exec spoke up. "Well, we just heard that Cal is an Excel Gee – I mean Excel Power User, right?"

I looked at my watch, "You have five seconds to decide; Cal or Tameeka? 5-4-3-2..."

All the execs began pointing at Cal.

"Cal!" "Cal!" "Cal!"

"Phew!" said Tameeka looking relieved. "Did we crash?"

"No," I said. "Cal crunched the numbers and saved the day."

The execs broke into applause for Cal, who jumped to his feet and took a mock bow. One exec yelled out, "Speech!"

Cal said, "Hero? I'm no hero. I only did what anyone with amazing Excel skills would do in this situation."

"Yes, you did, Cal," I said, "And it was a picture-perfect landing on – Uranus."

Cal pointed around the room, "And now all of you owe me your lives. Payback's a – "

"Right," I said, "And upon safe return to earth, Tameeka took a few months to boost her TQ. Fifteen short years later, she became CEO of DroneZone."

"Wow!" said Harold. "Hope you'll let us keep our jobs."

"I'll think about it," said Tameeka.

"Any more concerns?" I enquired.

Maria raised her hand, "Yes, I have one concern. If we roll out The Hamster Revolution, our success will hinge on our people's ability to grow and change. Is TQ something that people are born with, or is it mostly developed through experience?"

Want more tech tips from Coach?
Sign up for his TQ blog!
https://www.getcontrol.net/blog

9

NATURE OR NURTURE?

I spoke slowly. "Is TQ the result of nature or nurture? I'd say it's 80% nurture."

"Why?" said Cal.

"Because unlike IQ, we have tremendous control over our TQ," I said.

"How exactly do you define TQ?"

"TQ is the ability to strategically learn, leverage, and share tech insights."

"Break that down for us," said Maria.

"Of course.

- **Strategic Learning** means we continuously search for new zip tips and strategies.
- **Leverage** means we practice zips so we can use them in the real world.
- **Share** means that we share zips with others.

"Learn, leverage, and share – it makes sense," said Dita."

"And these abilities are not set in stone at birth," I said.

"What about you?" said Maria, "Did TQ come easy to you?"

"No. Earlier in my career, I struggled. Then, I had the good fortune to bump into Lenny and Jo. I was working at a Fortune 50 healthcare company. I was on a team with Lenny and Jo that was developing a huge slide presentation for the CEO. Those two co-workers – they worked so fast. Their fingers were a blur, and they produced twice as many slides as me."

"Did you ask for help?" said Maria.

"It never occurred to me," I replied. "It seems crazy now, but I was intimidated by them."

"Oh, I know that feeling," said Claire.

"But, I was holding the group back – and that felt awful. Then, it happened. Lenny and Jo took me to lunch and showed me twenty incredible shortcuts. They started with *Control + Z, X, C, V,* and moved on to a slew of presentation design ideas.

They showed me how to compose and animate slides. A whole new world opened up for me. I became a sponge. My TQ skyrocketed, especially when I began to realize how fun it was to share zip tips with my colleagues."

Maria smiled. "So, you went from worst to first."

"And," said Claire playfully, "became a tech rock star."

"Uh-huh. Lenny and Jo changed everything for me," I said. "And that's' how I know that Techsperts aren't born – they're developed. I'm living proof."

10

GO OR NO GO?

Maria stood up and said breezily. "Claire, thanks for organizing this summit. I'm afraid we're out of time. I motion to schedule a virtual meeting to further explore the Hamster Revolution for TQ. All in favor, say Aye!"

The room erupted in a chorus of *Ayes*.

"Is it unanimous?" asked Claire.

The execs looked around the room. Everyone's eyes settled on Cal.

"No way," he said.

Groans rang out. Cal always went against the grain. I think that's why I was starting to like him so much.

"I'm not in favor of continuing the discussion," he said.

"No?" I said, feeling a bit discouraged.

"I think the people in this room still have no idea what it's like to go through the TQ process. Coach, we can't take your word for it."

"We could talk to references," offered Dita.

"He could cherry-pick references," said Cal defiantly, "It's too risky."

"So, you're voting no?" said Claire, "You understand our investors want us to solve this problem, right?"

"I do," said Cal.

The room fell silent.

"I can't see this TQ stuff working," said Cal pausing for effect, "and for me, seeing is believing."

Claire looked up. "And?"

"If you want something done right, you have to do it yourself."

Dita looked worried. "We've been trying to do it ourselves for five years, Cal."

"You don't get it, people," said Cal motioning at me.

"Get what?" asked Harold.

"I'm very skeptical about this hamster guy."

"Maybe we can meet one-on-one?" I suggested, "and I could address your concerns."

"There are talkers and doers," continued Cal. "And I'm a

doer. You say the TQAT will roar like a lion – well, I think it might be an old stuffed animal."

Cal glared at me, and we locked eyes for an instant. And then I noticed a little glint in his eye, and I could have sworn he winked. Suddenly it hit me. Cal wasn't walking away from TQ; he was embracing it!

"If you're serving hamster food to 10,000 people, you better know what it tastes like!" he said.

Cal gestured at me. "Before we sit through another meeting with this guy, I think we should all take the TQAT first. And that includes Tameeka. We have to do a pilot to make sure we don't get burned."

"Whew!" I said, "I'm 110% on board with Cal's plan."

Everyone heaved a sigh of relief and broke into a round of applause.

I walked to the front of the room, "Let's reconvene after you all take the TQAT, and I'll provide an accelerated version of the TQ training experience via virtual meeting, OK?"

The execs were all in agreement with the pilot.

Maria nodded to Claire, who stood up, "Thank you all for coming to **The Digital Transformation Task Force** Summit at Camelback mountain. This meeting is officially adjourned."

11

TQ TIPS FOR VIRTUAL MEETINGS

I sat in my home office in the coastal town of Guilford, Connecticut, staring out the window at the sun sparkling on the calm waters of Long Island Sound. In the distance, a blue lobster boat made its way across the harbor, while above, an osprey cruised majestically through the air, searching for fish below.

I turned to face my two large, curved computer monitors and began to work through my virtual meeting checklist.

First, I shut down and restarted my PC. I did a quick bandwidth speed test and then pulled up the DroneZone home page to learn more about the company. In a virtual world, it's harder to build relationships. Showing a meeting guest that you're surfing their site sends a message that you care.

I sent a Do Not Disturb text to my family and turned off notifications on my PC, iPhone, and Apple Watch. I also locked my office door.

Next, I launched the web meeting, entered the pre-meeting

room, opened the plastic privacy cover of my webcam, and took a moment to check my lighting and framing.

The dazzling sun behind me caused my face to be shrouded in shadows, so I closed the blinds and turned on two soft front lights. I adjusted the webcam, so my head was centered in the top half of the screen, donned a sports coat, and entered the virtual meeting.

As always, I was twenty minutes early and the first to arrive. I shared my desktop and loaded a dynamic cover slide so that when my guests arrived, they would see a professional, positive, branded image along with my smiling face on the webcam. As always, each step of my pre-meeting checklist made me feel more and more relaxed and confident.

One by one, the familiar faces of Maria, Claire, Harold, and all the DroneZone execs began to fill the screen. Everyone seemed excited to discuss TQ.

They had completed the TQAT. Now it was time to start the pilot.

"Thank you so much for coming, everyone," said Claire. "And as the head of the Digital Transformation Task Force, I also want to thank you all for participating in this pilot. Coach, take it away."

"Thanks, Claire. Hi, everyone!" I said. "Before we begin to learn about our TQ profiles, I'd like to state the objective of this meeting, which is to provide a TQ pilot that increases your TQ by 30%. A couple of points:

1. Remember, we are condensing the program from a half-day to one hour due to your busy schedules.

2. This session itself will be an example of TQ virtual meeting best practices. Please pay attention to how I facilitate the meeting.

If you agree with all that I just said, please type the letter y into the chatbox."

It took a moment, but soon the entire group typed a y.

"Thanks, everyone. Since we'll be working together on this pilot, I think it would be nice to get to know each other a little better. Please type the name of your favorite movie into the chat."

I typed The Shawshank Redemption and then scanned the screen to see what everyone else had chosen.

Claire: Pride and Prejudice
Dita: The Pursuit of Happyness
Maria: The Social Network
Harold: The Princess Bride
Tameeka: Hidden Figures
Cal: The Godfather

One of the other execs surprised everyone with his choice: Finding Nemo. The virtual icebreaker worked its magic. The group immediately loosened up and began discussing and debating each other's picks.

When things quieted down, I asked, "Did anyone learn something new about a colleague?" Type y into the chat to respond."

Several executives typed a y.

"Good, "I said. "The way I'm using chat is a TQ best practice. Early interaction encourages everyone to participate throughout the meeting. It also prevents Hugos."

"Hugos?" said Claire.

"Hugos are awkward virtual meeting moments. A Hugo happens when two people start talking at once – then pause, and say, you go, no, you go.'"

"Happens all the time," said Claire.

"Those awkward Hugo moments come with a price. People become less and less likely to chime in – you lose engagement. Therefore, I'm encouraging you to be chat champions; this means that you promote a healthy discussion via chat throughout the meeting.

"Isn't that distracting?" asked Maria.

"We've discovered that it keeps people focused on business vs. drifting off to social media, email, or the web.

"You're packing quite a few virtual meeting zips into this session," observed Harold.

"Helpful?" I asked.

"Extremely."

"Would you like me to record the session so that everyone can review the facilitation tips?"

"Yes," said Maria, Claire, and Harold in unison. Other execs typed a y into the chatbox. Dita typed, yay!

"OK. Thank you all for taking the TQAT. Let's look at how the team did overall."

I shared my desktop and brought up an XY chart covered in blue dots.

Drone Zone Executive Team TQ Baseline

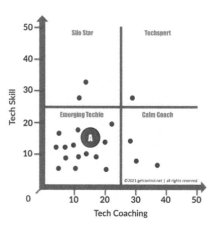

"Each one of these twenty dots represents the TQ score for a member of this team."
"Which one is me?" asked Cal.

"I'll get to that in just a sec. What do you think the big A circle represents?"

"Our average score?" ventured Tameeka.

"Exactly."

"So, we can see and compare improvement for individuals *and* teams?" asked Claire.

"The TQAT allows leaders to view digital transformation across the organization. With TQ, there is always a clear start and finish line."

"Finish line?" said Cal.

I advanced the slide, and all the blue dots danced across the screen into new positions. I could see everyone lean forward at once.

Drone Zone Executive Team 30% Gain Simulation

Before   **After**

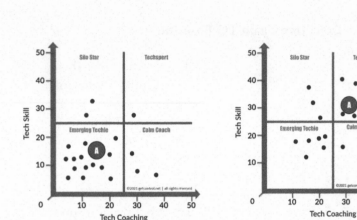

"Wowzers," said Harold. "We can see the change."

"Like never before," said Claire.

"This simulation shows a projected 30% increase in your team's TQ – that's our goal," I said. "Notice that some dots move – others, not so much."

"Now we can find the laggards and crack the whip," said Cal.

"Or find the tech-savvy ones and recruit them to mentor others," murmured Claire.
"Right," I said. "Your people's natural inclination to do well

– will be stimulated by seeing themselves on the TQ Chart."

"I've got a question," said Tameeka. "Let's say I work hard, and my score goes up. What does that do for me?"

"In addition to demonstrating tech proficiency to your entire team, you will save time and get more done."

"How much time?"

"To answer Tameeka's question, let's hold a little competition. I'd like everyone to type the answer to this question into the chat."

I displayed a slide that read:

TQ Initiative Stats

The Average Time Saved Per Participant is___ Days a Year.

The group looked interested.

I did my best to imitate a game show host.

"Whoever is closest to the correct answer wins a free, *imaginary* iPad 14."

"My *imaginary* boyfriend's going to love this," joked

Tameeka.

"I'm seeing the same guy," said Claire. "Rich, sharp dresser - and non-existent.

We all laughed. The group typed their guesses into the chat. I could tell they were keen on winning.

"Come on," said Claire, "the bets are in – who won?"

I advanced the slide and said, "The survey said...10 days a year![vi]"

The group gasped.

"That's a ton of time," I said. "And our winner is Tameeka!"

We took a quick moment to applaud Tameeka, who typed woo-hoo into the chatbox.

"Does everyone see how these chat techniques are making this meeting more fun and engaging?"

Without any prompt, the execs all typed y into the chatbox.

"Here's another question: Could these techniques make all DroneZone meetings more productive?"

Many attendees typed y in the chat.

"Wonderful. Well, folks, the big moment has arrived. It's time to review your TQ Profiles."

12

THE TQX AWARDS

"We all search for epic, life-changing moments," I said. "I believe discovering your TQ Profile, TQ score, and TQ Action Plan – can change your life."

"Um," said Cal. "Is this a cult initiation?"

"Yes, it is," I said with a smile.

I had come to enjoy jousting with Cal. He was tough but fair.

"For the first time, you'll be able to see your TQ score and tech type relative to your peers. Each participant will receive a description of their profile, advice on how to work with other tech types, and a post-training action plan."

"When do we get all that?" asked Harold.

"You'll receive an email right after this meeting."

"To make it fun, with your permission, I'll highlight one DroneZone executive for each of the four TQ profiles. I want to thank each of these leaders. Your reactions and feedback will help everyone better understand each tech type.

The first profile that we'll review is The Emerging Techie. And our first leader is Claire."

Claire winced, "Uh-oh. Can you highlight someone else?"

"Don't worry," I said, "you're actually in the best position to win it all."

"Win what?"

"The TQX Delta Award. It goes to the participant who achieves the biggest net increase in their TQ score."

"Award?" said Harold.

Claire paused for a moment. "So, you've gamified TQ?"

"Clever," said Harold. "A little recognition goes a long way."

Maria asked, "What does the X stand for?"

"X-cellence," I said. "Now that we can track TQ, we can gamify the initiative to boost interest. We present the awards at the end."

"This team is ultracompetitive," said Maria.

Cal took an interest.

"Are there other awards?" he said.

"Yes," I said. Here's a summary slide:

TQ Excellence (TQX) Awards

The TQX Awards

First, we have the Delta Award. Delta is Latin for change. It goes to the most improved participant. Emerging Techies often win this award because they —"

"Start at the bottom of the barrel?" asked Claire.

"That's not how I would describe it," I said. "We also give awards for
- The Top TQ Score
- Anyone Who Attains Techspert Status
- Completion of the TQ Action Plan

"Now you're talking," said Cal.

Maria shouted, "Let the TQX games begin!"

Want more tech tips from Coach?
Sign up for his blog!
https://www.getcontrol.net/blog

13

THE EMERGING TECHIE

 "Let's get back to exploring Claire's TQ profile, The Emerging Techie."

Claire sunk in her seat, "Uh oh. Back to me."

"Like most of you, Claire is an Emerging Techie. Please give her a big virtual round of applause by typing an 'a' into the chatbox."

The chatbox lit up:

a	Doug
a	Bev
a	Harold
a	Gary
aaa, better you than me!	Dita
a	Tameeka
aa	Wanda
a my condolences	Cal
a	Dave
a I am probably an ET too	Aara

"Applause? For what?" asked Claire, "Being rubbish with technology?"

The Emerging Techie

"Why do you feel that way?" I said.

"I'm terrible at managing my inbox. I still use a paper to-do list, and I've been reduced to tears installing an ink cartridge on my printer."

"Those challenges," I said, "are surprisingly surmountable."

"Do you reckon?" said Claire.

"Emerging Techies make up 65% of all professionals. They score lower on both Tech and Coaching."

"That's most employees," observed Harold. "You're in good company, Claire."

"Exactly, Harold. With an average TQ of 30, Emerging Techies often—

"30?" gasped Claire. "That's a failing grade!"

"Not on the TQ scale," I said. "That will soon be clear."

"OK," she replied, "continue the torture."

"Well, I was about to say that many Emerging Techies are very successful people. They have other talents like customer relationships, design expertise, or public speaking."

"Claire is a great public speaker," said Maria.

"I'm not surprised," I said. "The problem is that all of these skills – even public speaking – are becoming more tech-driven."

"There's no escape. I'm trapped," sighed Claire.

I moved the slide forward to show Claire's score on the XY grid.

"Claire is actually in the top 30% of Emerging Techies. She may be able to help other Emerging Techies right from the start."

"I doubt it," said Claire.

"We recommend that Emerging Techies spend 80% of their time working on tech skills and just 20% on boosting coaching skills. It's important to get comfortable with at least twenty zip tips before sharing them with the world."

"Well," said Claire, "That takes some of the pressure off."

"Now, let's take a closer look at your profile, Claire. Here are some Emerging Techie characteristics that we've uncovered via focus groups.

- Emerging Techies are often nervous about changing settings or trying new features.
- They view digital shortcuts and templates as tricky to use.
- Emerging Techies often learn a tech tip but struggle to recall it months later, when they need it most.
- In some cases, they've suffered a significant career setback as a result of a tech glitch.
- They may justify tech avoidance by telling themselves that they're too busy.

The Emerging Techie

- Emerging Techies often believe that it's useless to learn a new zip because it may be obsolete tomorrow.

"Things are changing so fast nowadays," said an exec.

"In my experience," I said, "the change is manageable. I use the same steps to create an email rule, as I did 20 years ago."

"Excel hasn't changed much either," said Cal.

"The bottom line is that Emerging Techies view TQ skills as a *bad investment*. The moment they start to see the investment paying off -- good things start to happen."

"I like good things," said Claire.

"Well, here's good news. Boosting TQ is easier than improving IQ or EQ. We can't go back and pick smarter, more well-adjusted parents, but we can commit to mastering 15 useful zips."

"So how do I begin my transformation from hapless hamster to talented Techspert?" asked Claire.

"Focus on three basic Emerging Techie strategies."

"Bracing for impact," grinned Claire.

"Strategy one, Stop the negative self-talk. You need a new mantra Claire."

"I do?"

"Yes. *I'm rubbish with technology*; it isn't very motivating."

"I thought it was kind of catchy."
"Perhaps, something a tad more optimistic might help?"

"Such as?"

"How about something simple like this,

I'm finding new zips all the time.

Say it."

"OK. *I'm finding new zips all the time.*"

"That wasn't so bad, was it?" said Maria, "Maybe add a little more oomph next time."

"Strategy two: Practice."

Cal looked skeptical. "Your best practice is – practice?"

"One of my favorite sayings is, *Repetition is the mother of all knowledge.* I'm recommending that Emerging Techies repeat each new zip five to ten times."

"Really?" asked Claire.

"Really. And here's an exercise to underscore this point." I turned to Dita. "How long have you had a smartphone?"

"About fifteen years, I guess."

"Did you know that the average professional receives 46 push notifications per day on their phone? That's over 250,000 interruptions over the last fifteen years.[vii]"

The Emerging Techie

"Seriously?" exclaimed Dita.

"It gets worse! According to a Microsoft study, every email interrupt slows your work pace for 10-15 minutes.[viii] Push notifications do the same – they steal your focus."

Tameeka nodded, "At school, we stop everything when our phones buzz. Then we look up and say, *Sorry, It was nothing*".

"We're all wasting time like that," said Harold.

"So, let's fight back. Take out your phones and tap *Settings > Notifications.* Find one app that sends you unnecessary notifications. Turn it off and share the app's name in the chat.

The execs got to work, and soon a bunch of apps appeared in the chat feed, including cooking, game, and music apps.

"Brilliant," I said. "Now repeat the whole process four more times."

"You mean I should go back to *Settings* and start over?" asked Cal.

"Right."

The execs followed my instructions.

"I feel like it's a bit easier each time," said Claire.

"And harder to forget?" I said.

"Uh-huh."

The execs worked diligently on the assignment.

"I have way more than five apps to turn off," typed Dita.

"Shut 'em down," I said. "Reclaim your focus. Keep going, everyone!"

The execs explored their phones vigorously.

"This is important. Repeat the process a few more times, but this time, look around the settings area and see if you can discover a new feature."

Everyone jumped into the new assignment. The execs looked like happy kids on a treasure hunt.

"Pop your discoveries into the chat. Anything new?"

"I've found ten apps I don't use," typed Maria.

"Zap 'em!" I ordered. "Press and hold the app, then tap x or Delete. Keep exploring.!"

After a couple of minutes, Claire typed, "What's *text replacement*?"

"It's an amazing feature, Claire. You can spell out long, complex phrases in just a couple of taps. Those of you with iPhones type *omw* and hit the spacebar."

"It says *On my way*," typed Dita. "Wow!"

I took a moment to guide the group through the text replacement feature. Within the span of a few minutes, everyone had:

- Cut distracting push notifications by 50%

The Emerging Techie

- Created five time-saving text replacements

"Type a y if you think you'll be using these zips for the rest of your career?"

"I can see that the Ys have it," I said, "Claire, did you find any of those tips hard to use?"

"Not harder than being CLO at DroneZone," she replied.

"Great. Our third Emerging Techie Strategy is: *Be a Tech Explorer.* Some of the best tech features are just out of sight. When Emerging Techies systematically track them down, they discover all kinds of shortcuts and time-saving features."

"But, where do we begin?" typed Dita.

"Don't worry, Dita, that's my job," I said. "Time for the Frankenstein exercise."

"Sounds scary," said Tameeka in the chat.

"I want you all to build a monstrous slide presentation. And here's the trick: Try to use as many presentation features as you can. You can insert objects, edit clip art, animate shapes, change the master slide, alter images, or create a hideous custom theme. Extra credit if your computer freezes from using so many features!"

"This is going to be ugly," said Tameeka.

"Ugly is good. If you find something new and useful, share it in the chat. "Ready, set, explore!"

After a few seconds, almost every exec was beaming, and the chatbox soon began to churn.

- I just realized that we could copy images by left-clicking on the object, pressing Control, and dragging my mouse to the side.

- I finally figured out the difference between animations and transitions.

- I learned how to insert **Cutout people** images. So cool!

As the exercise ended, everyone was buzzing about one discovery or another. I paused to enjoy the vibrant sound of TQ in action.

"I'm glad you had fun creating your monsters," I said.

"It was brilliant," said Maria. "I'm learning so much today."

"Here's one more exploration exercise called Turning the Stones."

"Huh?" said Cal.

"From now on, Emerging Techies must leave no tech stone unturned. They must start to click on any icon that stands for *More options* to see what lies beneath."

"Such as," said Harold.

"I want you to click on every gear, ellipsis, and nine-dot icon you can find. Those are your TQ stones."

"Let me guess," typed Dita. "You've got a TQ exercise for us?"

"Of course. We're getting to know each other so well. Open any app on your PC, then find and click on as many stones as possible. Type any new features you find into the chatbox. Ready, set, go!"

At first, everyone seemed hesitant.

"Start looking," I said encouragingly. "Go on, get into the stone zone."

After a few minutes, several execs discovered new and useful features."

"Hey," said Dita, "I found a three-dot button next to a contact in 365 Teams. I hovered over the contact, and there it was!"

"And?"

"I found the *Notify when available* option. This feature alerts me when a contact changes their status from ***Do Not Disturb*** to ***Available***."

"So what?"

"Well, if I have an important question for Maria, I can reach out to her when she's available to chat."

"That's tech-driven time management in action," I said, "OK, everyone, has this exercise been useful?"

As I had expected, the execs loved what they had learned in just a few short minutes.

"These tips are great," typed one exec, "But are they for everyone? Some of us are not Emerging Techies."

"That's OK," I said, "While these tips benefit Emerging Techies the most – if it makes you say *Wow!* then try the tip out."

"Will do!"

"So Emerging Techies, start building monsters and looking under stones. OK?"

"Definitely," said Claire, sounding more assertive than before. She laughed and said, "I'm feeling better about my tech type."

"Why?"

"I guess it's because *I'm finding new zips all the time.*"

Zip Tip Exercise: Smartphone Text Replacement

iPhone Autotexting
- Tap *Settings* > *General* > *Keyboard* > *Text Replacement*

- Tap the **+** *sign* > Place the longer phrase next to *Phrase*

- Place your trigger phrase next to *Shortcut*

Samsung Galaxy Text Replacement

- Tap *Settings* > *General management* > *Language and input*

- Tap **On-screen keyboard** > *Samsung Keyboard*

- Tap **Smart typing** > *Text Shortcuts* > *Add* > Place trigger phrase under *Add shortcut* and longer phrase under *Expanded phrase* > Tap *Add.*

Need more tech tips from Coach?
*Text **tqtips** to **22828***
and get a zip each month!

14

THE SILO STAR

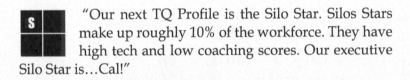 "Our next TQ Profile is the Silo Star. Silos Stars make up roughly 10% of the workforce. They have high tech and low coaching scores. Our executive Silo Star is...Cal!"

"A Silo Star is born!" said Maria in the chat.

"Hey! I'm a self-made man," said Cal.

"You need to start sharing your TQ brilliance," said Dita.

"You're on your own," replied Cal.

"Well, that pretty much reflects the Silo Star's old mantra," I said, "*I'm keeping it all to myself.*"

"And what's my new mantra, Coach?" asked Cal, puffing out his lip like a sad toddler. "Sharing is caring?"

Everyone erupted into laughter.

"Close," I said. "How about *Dare to share the magic.*"

The Silo Star

Cal grinned and typed, "Oh, now I'm supposed to be David Copperfield?"

"Cal, your zips do seem like magic to your colleagues. You wave your mouse and – presto – a hard task gets done in half the time."

"The amazing Caldini," typed Harold.

Cal looked a bit miffed. "Listen," he said, "I'm the CFO of a big company in hot water. Frankly, I don't have time for this."

"Cal has a point," said Maria. "I need him focused on finance every day."

"Don't get me wrong," said Cal, "I get as frustrated as the next guy when I see how clueless people can be."

"So, what bugs you most, Cal?" I said.

"Where do I begin? Take something as simple as a browser like Edge or Chrome. People open them and search for the same sites repeatedly. Why don't they have their three or four most-used sites automatically open when they launch their browser? All they have to do is click the *Settings* gear! And tell me this, why do so many people have just three shortcuts on their bookmark bar when they could have thirty! I call them long-cutters!"

"Would anyone like to see Cal's browser zips?" I said.

The execs filled the chatbox with strident demo requests.

"Cal," I said. "Can you show us your zips?"

"OK, Just let me open my -" Cal froze for a moment. "Oh, I see your little game," he said.

"Game?" I asked.

"Suddenly, I'm Coach Cal -- breaking out of my silo – taking the time to share browser tips and tricks. Well, I'll play along, but I still maintain that I'm way too busy for this stuff."

"Understood."

"Toss me the presentation, then."

I did, and Cal walked the group through several ways to optimize browsers to save time and get more done. As he shared each tip, I could tell he was beginning to enjoy the positive responses in the chat."

"That was brilliant," I said. "I even learned a few new things myself."

"Has the master become the student?" asked Harold.

"Happily."

"And I'll admit that was pretty painless," said Cal. "Now, I can sleep at night knowing Frank from manufacturing has finally clawed his way onto the information superhighway."

"But you still haven't got time for this?" I asked.

"Nope. Too busy."

"I have an idea, Cal. Since your PC is already on the screen, would you mind if I walked you through a possible TQ solution for your time issue?"

"Uh, OK," said Cal warily.

"Great. The entire organization could benefit from Cal's tip, right? So, let's make a video."

"I don't have time to produce videos," protested Cal.

"This will only take a minute."

"Alright," he replied in a voice that reminded me just a bit of Eeyore from Winnie the Poo.

"Thanks, Cal. So, let's make a video using the desktop version of PowerPoint. Here are the steps –follow along.

- Create a new, blank presentation.

- Click *Insert > Screen Recording* on the far-right side of the ribbon. See? A control panel appears at the top-center.

- Use the *Cross tool* to select the recording area.

- Click the *Record button* and narrate your tips.

- When you're done, move your mouse to the top-center, so the control panel reappears, and tap the *Stop* button.

Cal followed my instructions. He reviewed his best practices and hit the *Stop* button.

"Interesting," he said. "The video popped into the slide."

"All you have to do is save the presentation and email a link to everyone here."

"Is my audio there as well?" asked Cal.

"Sure is."

"Cal," said Maria, "I'd like to share that tip with everyone."

"Maybe I should polish it up a bit?"

"We're in the YouTube era," I said, "Useful content beats slick production."

"It's fine, Cal," added Harold. "You did great."

Cal saved the video to SharePoint and emailed the link to Maria. Then she sent the link and a brief message crediting Cal to all 10,000 DroneZone employees. Seconds later, the executives noticed the video in their inboxes.

"I'm watching it now, Cal," said Dita, "I'm recommending that our salespeople use your ideas to create links to their Sales Lead and Opportunity pages in the CRM."

Suddenly, positive reviews from all over DroneZone began to roll in. The executives read a few of the emails to each other.

- We can use this to bookmark safety protocols
- My assistant is going to bookmark calendars

The Silo Star

Cal and the executives seemed bewildered.

"What – just – happened?" said Claire slowly.

"TQ," I said. "Maria and Cal just helped 10,000 people work better, smarter, and faster. Now I'd recommend planning out our next company-wide zip tip blast a bit more."

"Got it," said Maria.

"Let's switch gears and help our Silo Stars get more relaxed with tech coaching. We recommend that Silo Stars dedicate 80% of their TQ time to developing their coaching skills."

"And 20% on learning new zips?" said Cal

"Yes," I said, "Silo Stars can't lose track of what elevated their game in the first place."

"Makes sense," said Harold. "I'm excited to see that silo door opening up."

"Silo Stars make incredible strides once they begin to hone their coaching and presentation skills. With that in mind, here are some coaching tips to get the ball rolling.

TQ Coaching Tips

Raise the Stakes
When sharing zips, always state the most significant benefit. Don't exaggerate, but make sure you explain why you love the tip."

"Can you give me an example," said Cal.

"Sure, rather than describing a zip as merely useful, I might say, this zip is saving me a ton of time in a specific area – like cleaning up your inbox."

Get to Wow
I fell in love with tech coaching when people began to show how much they loved the zips. So, think about how you can dramatize each zip.

For example, when I demonstrate auto texting in Microsoft Word, I enlarge the text to make it easier to see. Then I fire off five of my best examples in rapid succession. I say *Bam!* for each one and explain why it helps me save time.

Use TQ Power Phrases
"Words matter. I've seen a few coaches struggle to get people interested because they chose the wrong language. Here are a few key phrases that I use:

- Here is the **easiest and most practical way** to organize your digital files.

- This search tip will help you find files **in a flash.**

- This email rule is a **simple way** to eliminate that inbox overload.

- When you **get more done, you have more fun.**

- I'm going to help you **get organized** once and for all.

Tech tips can be exciting or boring. That's why it pays to practice using the right words.

Show Different Ways to Use Each Zip
If you show twenty-five zips at a coaching session, your audience will start to feel overwhelmed. Instead, share five zips but cover three variations for each one. People will remember more if you share less.

Go Slow
Silo Stars often move too fast when sharing a zip tip. Remember, your audience is seeing your advice for the first time. So, go slow and repeat the steps if you feel you lost anyone."

Emotions First – Zips Second
"Our minds remember emotional experiences. So always begin by emphasizing the most significant pain points before you show the solution.

For example, *Don't you hate back-to-back meetings? It's incredibly stressful when a meeting ends at ten, and the next one starts at ten. How does that make you feel?*"

Everyone groaned.

"Horrible," typed Harold.

"Once you've evoked the frustration of back-to-back meetings, your audience will be dying to know how to set your eCalendar default meeting time to 50 minutes."

"You can?" said Maria.

"In Google Calendar too," asked Tameeka.

"Of course," I said and quickly showed the group this simple setting change.

"When you dare to share, you're growing as a manager and leader. You're stepping up to the plate and helping the entire organization grow. Of course, increasing your Tech Coaching score will bump you into the Techspert quadrant in record time. OK?"

There was a moment of silence. I crossed my fingers under my desk and thought, *wait for it*.

Finally, Cal spoke up. "I guess I can *Dare to share a little magic* now and then."

I smiled. "Bravo. You're going to love it."

"Let's not get crazy," said Cal.

Zip Tip Exercise: Set 10 Minute Meeting Buffer

Outlook Calendar
- Click *File > Options > Scroll to calendar options*
- Set *End Appts* to 10 minutes early *> OK*

Google Calendar
- Go to Google Calendar, Click *Gear > Settings*
- Click *Event Settings > Set Default duration to 50 minutes >* Check *Speedy meetings* checkbox

*See Cal's browser tip video at getcontrol.net/cal

15

THE CALM COACH

 "Our third TQ Profile is the Calm Coach. And our executive match is Tameeka. Type an a to give her a big round of virtual applause.

"Hey," said Tameeka, "I'm just an intern."

"Yet here you are," I said with a wink. "Calm Coaches like Tameeka make up 20% of the workforce. They have low tech and high coaching scores. We recommend that they spend 60% of their effort in building tech skills and 40% on coaching skills."

I advanced the presentation to a slide showing a businessman sitting in the lotus position.

"I'll have what he's having," said Dita.

"Like this guy," I continued, "the Calm Coach is cool, calm, and collected around technology. Unlike the Emerging Techie, a Calm Coach feels relaxed about learning new tech skills. They understand that they need to know more about digital tools like email, chat, or search.

"It sounds like they're looking forward to it," said Claire.

"All they need is clear guidance. The Calm Coach's challenge is: Where do I start? That's why their beginning mantra is: *What's the plan?*

Unlike the Silo Star, the Calm Coach enjoys sharing tech insights. They're more extroverted than Emerging Techies or Silo Stars."

"Tameeka represents one kind of Calm Coach. I believe that her school uses Google Docs and that most of her fellow students use Macs. Right, Tameeka?"

"Pretty much," she replied.

"But at DroneZone, you switched over to 365 and a PC. Do you miss your Mac?"

"Yeah, the change threw me off. All the buttons were in different places and had different names. There is no Command button on a PC. It also took me a while to figure out that Outlook rules are the same thing as Gmail filters."

"Did you create a lot of Gmail filters back at school?"

"Just a few."

"Were they useful?"

"Sort of. I need to learn how filters work in 365."

"But eventually, you'll figure it out."

"Sure. But I might have a question or two."

"That's fine. You see, Tameeka embodies many characteristics of a Calm Coach. She's at ease with technology but needs a little time and help to boost those tech skills."

"Let's take a moment to review how to create rules in Outlook. There are many ways. Here is one of the easiest."

I popped my inbox on the screen. "To autoroute all messages from a sender to an email folder, go to your Outlook inbox > *Right-click* on an email from that sender > Click *Rules* > *Create Rules* > Check the *top and bottom boxes* > Then double-click on your preferred destination email folder. That's it."

"Great!" said Dita as she jotted the steps down, "Got it!"

"But I recommend that you don't autoroute important senders' emails to a folder because you can easily miss a high priority message. Use the Outlook Search folder feature for that."

"Tameeka," said Cal, "I use Google docs at home. Can you show us how to create a rule in Gmail?"

"Um," said Tameeka. "Sure,"

Tameeka shared her desktop, opened a browser, and logged into Gmail.

"From the Gmail inbox," she said,

- Click on an email from the sender you want to route

- At the top-center of the screen, click the *three-dot More options* button

- Click *Filter messages like these* > Click *Create filter*

- Check the *Skip the Inbox box* and then check the *Apply label* box

- Select or create a label and click *Create filter*."

"Impressive," said Cal. "So, you're interning for Harold?"

"Yeah."

"Any interest in finance?"

"Hey, Cal, said Harold good-naturedly, "stop trying to steal my interns."

The group laughed at the jousting between the two execs.

"There are many other kinds of Calm Coaches," I explained. "Some are IT wizards who know how to code but never paid much attention to standard-issue technology. Some are trainers who aren't very tech-savvy, but they're quick studies who love to create *Wow!* moments."

"And this class seems to have a *Wow!* moment, every ten seconds," said Harold.

"So, what can Tameeka do to boost TQ?" asked Claire.

"Study the Calm Coach Action Plan and master about a dozen tech tips. The next step is to put all those zips into a dynamic, well-rehearsed twenty-minute presentation. I call it the TQ Setlist."

The Calm Coach

"You mean, like a pop band's setlist?" asked Harold.

"Exactly. I played in a band for many years, and the setlist was crucial. We played great songs in just the right order. We needed to bring the crowd's energy up and down to keep them engaged. The same thing is true of zip tips."

"So," said Maria, "each zip is like a song?"

"Right. Once the Calm Coach gets the set down, they can begin teaching colleagues. We recommend they start with a receptive group of Emerging Techies. It usually takes just a few weeks for them to get rolling."

"Does it all just click into place?" said Harold.

"Well, once a Calm Coach shares their setlist ten or fifteen times, they get into a zone. They work on their delivery and start to get more frequent and enthusiastic *Wows!*"

"And then they're hooked," said Claire. "When a teacher delivers an *aha* moment – it feels great."

"My question is," said Tameeka, "how do I get started? I mean, what zips should I learn first?"

"Let me give you a head start, Tameeka. I've been teaching zips for twenty years – and I'd like to share my TQ setlist with you. Think of it as a starting point."

"Awesome."

"I usually start with these zips

The Coach's TQ Setlist

1. Advanced email search
2. Transform an email into a calendar item
3. Create an email rule
4. Various smartphone tips
5. Discuss effective e-Communication
6. Demonstrate text replacement on phone and pc
7. Create email and pc templates
8. Advanced smartphone dictation tips

"Fantastic!" said Tameeka.

"The TQ action plan you're about to receive via email will guide you to videos for each zip. Then, it's up to you."

Tameeka addressed Harold. "Do you mind if I work on this during my internship?"

"Not at all," said Harold. "In the long run, you'll be more productive, and I frankly hope that you can share your TQ setlist with our whole team."

I forwarded the slide and added, "Here are some questions you can ask yourself as you practice your set.

- What's the best order for these zips?
- How can I bring each zip to life?
- How can I get them to say *Wow!*
- How can we make the session more interactive?

- How can I smoothly transition from one zip to the next?"

"Got it," said Tameeka, taking notes on her PC.

"I would also encourage you to find a few Emerging Techies for a test run or dress rehearsal. Pay close attention to their reactions. Try to home in on sweet spots that make them say *Wow!*"

"Sign me up," said Tameeka.

"Spoken like a true Calm Coach," said Claire.

"Your new mantra is: *Master the zips and build a list*. Now that you have a plan, it's all up to you."

"One question," said Tameeka.

"Fire away."

"I'm great with dictation, but what do you mean by advanced dictation?"

"Advanced dictation will help you double the speed and accuracy of writing anything on a mobile device. So, take out your phones, and let's try something fun."

I plugged a USB cable into my phone, and suddenly my iPhone home page appeared on the web meeting screen.

"How are you doing that?" asked Harold.

"It's an app called apowermirror, but before you use it, you must get permission from your IT help desk."

"I get it, said Harold, "security comes first!"

The execs pulled out their phones.

"Now open an email and tap into the body of the message. When I count to three, tap your phone's dictation button and hold it up to your headphone or PC speaker so that it can hear my voice."

I could see the execs getting ready to go.

"Here we go! 1-2-3...tap!"

I hit the microphone icon and began to speak.

"Hi Claire (comma) (new paragraph)

Request (colon) Please send feedback on today's TQ presentation. (new paragraph)
(dash dash) We are hoping to understand what you liked and what can be improved (period) (new paragraph)

(dash dash) The initiative can be customized to fit your culture, values, and mission (period) (smiley face)

(dash dash) Any questions (question mark)

I completed the dictation by tapping the microphone icon. The result was an easy-to-read, bullet-pointed message.

"Mine came out great," said Tameeka.

"All good?" I asked, glancing at the webcams. The execs nodded, and some held up their phones.

The Calm Coach

"All I did was:

1. Say all *punctuation* like colon, question mark, or exclamation point
2. Say *dash dash* to create bullet points
3. And say *new paragraph* to add line spaces

Using advanced dictation is an easy way to craft clear, concise, and actionable mobile messages."

"I noticed that you paused for a long time at one point," observed Cal.

"You have plenty of time to think about what to say next. That also improves the quality of communication."

Dita said, "Funny, I recall that dictation used to cut me off if I paused."

"That was probably Siri. Smartphone assistants time out fast, making it almost impossible to collect your thoughts. That's why I recommend the basic dictation feature on iPhones and Androids."

"Does advanced dictation work for all mobile apps?" asked Harold.

"That's why it's so powerful. You can use it in a mobile document, web page, text, email, or chat message. Now here's a final exercise. Pick a partner and exchange a few advanced dictation texts. Use all three advanced techniques. It will take you less than twenty minutes to improve your dictation skills."

I could see that the execs were sending messages back and forth with excellent results.

"So, there you have it, Tameeka," I said. "Your path forward is to master your TQ setlist and concentrate on expanding your already strong mobile skills."

She folded her arms and, in a determined voice, said, "I'm going to *master the zips and build my list.*

16

THE TECHSPERT

Our final profile is the Techspert. This tech type possesses high tech and high coaching skills. Only 3% of the workforce qualify for this tech type. When I think of the Techspert, I see **The Future of Work** and leadership too. It's a tech type to which we all should aspire.

Techsperts spend 50% of their TQ time on skills and 50% on coaching. They explore the technosphere, find useful tools, master them, and then share them with their colleagues.

I visualize them as a positive wave of productivity rippling through organizations. Sadly, the Techspert is often an unsung hero, whose contributions are not recognized by leadership."

"Until now," said Maria. "The TQAT shines a light on them."

"Who is our Techspert," said Claire, "I'm dying to know."

"OK...It's...Harold!"

"I knew it," said Dita.

"Wow," said Harold. "Not sure how that happened."

"It's fixed!" joked Cal.

"Now that I think about it," noted Dita, "Harold has given me lots of great advice about technology."

Harold typed ty into the chat.

"Congrats, Harold," I said. There are two Techspert classifications: green belt and black belt. Harold just barely squeaked into the green belt category – but that is still an outstanding achievement. You'll receive a TQ certificate for this accomplishment."

"What's the difference between a green belt and a black belt?" asked Cal.

"To be certified as a TQ black belt, Harold would need to go through advanced training and pass a final exam. Black belts are approved to teach all TQ classes. They often become in-house TQ trainers."

"Maybe you should go for it, Harold," suggested Maria.

"We'll see," said Harold. "I'm pretty sure I just barely made it to green belt."

"That's true," I said. "You're right on edge. Now, all Techsperts know that continuous learning is needed to sustain and improve Techspert status."

"What else can you tell us about this profile," said Claire.

"The Techspert is usually a highly productive and valued

colleague. Here are a few common traits:

- Techsperts are curious, passionate, and energetic
- They view TQ as a strategic imperative for all
- Techsperts often become respected leaders
- They find novel uses for basic tech tools

"Like using text replacement to spell out long phrases?" said Dita.

"That's a classic Techspert workaround," I said. "Another example is Google 100."

Cal held up his hand, "Hold it. Google what?"

"100. Yeah, you can set Google to pull up 100 search results instead of just 10. The setting change allows you to quickly scroll through ten times more results without clicking on the next o in Gooooogle at the bottom of the screen."

I demonstrated a Google 100 search for the group, and the chat filled up with requests to further explain the zip. I copied and pasted a link into the chatbox to kick-off a quick learn-by-doing exercise.

https://www.google.com/search?num=100

"Go ahead," I said, "Click on the link and search."

Within a minute, all the participants had done their first Google 100 search. Positive reviews begin to pop into the chat.

"So how do you use this feature?" said Harold.

"Well," I said, "I used it before this meeting to research some of you."

"You did?" said Maria, putting on a look of mock horror. "And what did you find out about me?"

"In addition to being a respected tech exec, you're an All-American distance runner in your age group. Harold's family fosters rescue dogs. And Cal is a scratch golfer who has won his club tournament three years in a row."

"Um," said Cal, "I won the tournament four years in a row."

"Congrats!" I replied.

"Our reps could use this technique to build relationships with customers," mused Dita.

"And R&D could use Google 100 to speed up research," said Maria.

"That's Techspert-like behavior," I said, " By the way, you can also change the setting in your Google account by searching once and then clicking **Settings > Search Settings >** and changing **Results per page** to 100."

"Awesome," said Tameeka.

"Now, where was I?" In all the excitement about search, I had lost my train of thought.

"You were describing the traits of a Techspert," said Cal.

"Ah…yes. Techsperts know the technosphere changes each

day. So, their current and future mantra will always be, *I have so much to learn.*"

"Really?" said Cal. "Aren't they the know-it-alls?"

"Quite the contrary - they're TQ sponges. They eagerly explore their apps and devices. They study upgrades and updates, looking for useful new features. They know that no single person can know-it-all."
"They're humble because there's so much to learn," said Claire.

"They see the world differently," I added. I advanced to a slide with a table. "Here's how different tech types view TQ."

TQ Profile Levels

Level	TQ Profile	Perspective
1	Emerging Techie	Tactical
2	Silo Star and Calm Coach	Strategic
3	Techspert	System

"At level one, the Emerging Techie has a tactical approach to technology. If someone shares a zip with them, they try to remember it – but that's about it."

"Interesting," murmured Maria.

"At level two, the Calm Coach and Silo Star take a more strategic approach. The Silo Star has steadily accumulated tech tips as a way of boosting job performance. The Calm Coach continuously strives to be a great teacher and communicator."
"I've never thought of myself like that," said Tameeka.

"Same with me," admitted Cal.

"Interesting, isn't it?" I said, "The Techspert sees that the **Technosphere** is a vast and mostly unmanaged system. Some would call them Systems Thinkers[ix] Techsperts view the **Digital Office** as a factory that takes in raw data and turns it into documents, decisions, and deliverables. Apps like Excel, Tableau, or Salesforce are the machinery that refines ideas and data into more useful information. A digital factory's goal is to convert data to info, info to knowledge, and knowledge to wisdom. But creating wisdom isn't enough. Each factory manager must effectively store all that insight in a well-organized digital file system."

"Or we lose it," mused Claire.

"This is a new way to look at our jobs," typed Dita.

"I'm glad you agree," I said, "Techsperts continuously ask for feedback and search for trends that can make their digital office more efficient. They view browsers, search tools, and shortcuts as vehicles that transport them around the technosphere.

They can spot a TQ bottleneck from a mile away. They understand that fuzzy labels on documents, disorganized folders, and lost passwords, gum up the works, adding friction to the system. Techsperts know that friction leads to procrastination and mistakes, so they fix those bottlenecks.

The Techspert is an early adopter. When Microsoft introduced Teams, Techsperts were eager to test and master it. They studied the new Planner app and began using it because it's far superior to Outlook Tasks. Then, they integrated the Planner app into a Teams Channel – and showed their colleagues a new, more tech-driven way to get work done."

"You lost me," said Claire, "What is Planner?"

"It's a new, 365 task management app that makes it incredibly easy to document and complete tasks. I can show you some innovative ways to use it next time. Would you like that?"

The execs all typed y into the chat.

Claire gulped, "Definitely. Does the black belt see the world differently?"

"They take an even higher-level view of the system. The TQ black belt's goal is to help every co-worker optimize their digital factory. They also try to help everyone, including clients and vendors, integrate their digital factories to create a wave of productive collaboration. They try to make everything…"

I paused to find the right word. "cohesive. And when a system becomes cohesive, you arrive at a whole new level of performance; I guess you could call it – **The Future of Work**."

I paused to take a sip of my home-brewed mochaccino. As the rich chocolate tannins worked their magic, I realized that we were all in a different headspace – gazing down at the workplace from a 10,000-foot view. I looked into my webcam and smiled. Twenty speechless executives stared back, riveted to their screens.

I could tell that our conversation was coming to an end. I let the executives know that a full-length session would have contained more zips, strategies, and a big discussion about how different tech types relate to each other.

I thanked them all for their participation. I felt energized and refreshed. The TQ discussion was always a stimulating one – and I loved seeing people react to the quantum leap forward made possible by the TQAT.

"The final thing that the Techspert understands is that **TQ should be fun**. It's fun to create a Frankenstein presentation and search for treasure under stones. It's a blast to use Google 100 search to find what you need fast. Finally, it's rewarding to hear someone say, *Wow! I never knew that!*"
I paused and took a deep breath.

"Thank you for having me. Can we work together to bring TQ to your people?"

Claire thanked me and addressed the team.

"So, what do you think?" she said.

"Sales needs TQ," said Dita.

"It simple, and it makes sense," said Harold, "I think it may be our best shot at getting DroneZone back on its feet. What do you think, Tameeka?"

"This is a big deal for anyone coming into the workplace," she replied, "I wish we had a TQ class at school."

"Cal?" said Claire glancing nervously at her stubborn colleague.
Cal gave the two thumbs down gesture, "Finance votes,"

suddenly, he flipped his hands 180 degrees, "Two thumbs way up!"

We all paused to see Maria's reaction. After all, as CEO, she had the final say.

She clasped her hands together, "Claire, it's your project; you are the final decision maker. If you decide to go forward with TQ, you've got my full support. I do have one request."

"What's that?" said Claire.

"I'd like you and three other L&D leaders to become certified black belts. That way, we can build a dedicated team of TQ ambassadors."

"You've got a deal," said Claire looking excited, "Thanks, everyone. I guess it's time to crack on – with TQ!"

Need more tech tips from Coach?
*Text **tqtips** to **22828***
and get a zip each month!

17

THE FUTURE OF WORK

Two years later.

As the Boeing 777X hurtled down the runway, I marveled at the power of technology. Technology had helped the world recover from a global health crisis, technology found a way to vault this 70-ton hunk of metal into the sky, and it had given me a beautiful mission in life.

I had spent the day in Raleigh, North Carolina, helping leaders at one of the world's biggest broadband companies apply TQ across the organization. The program had been a big success, and I was glad now to be able to relax and gather my thoughts.

Soon we were flying over the Carolina coastline, and I could make out the beaches and small towns of the Outer Banks, a popular vacation destination. The plane tilted slightly as it began to turn north towards JFK. I was homeward bound.

Staring absentmindedly out of the window, I couldn't help but think that a little over a hundred years ago, the Wright brothers labored below on the dunes of Kitty Hawk, struggling to achieve the miracle of controlled flight. Once they succeeded, like true Techsperts, they shared their incredible insight with the world.

I settled into my seat, popped my noise-canceling headset on, and cued up a podcast that I'd been longing to hear all day. Tim Furnace, the host of the world's most popular technology series, had interviewed Claire. Millions of listeners would stream the show and discover how TQ had transformed DroneZone in two short years.

I felt emotional as I listened to Claire bubbling with enthusiasm. I smiled when I heard her tell Tim Furnace, "You know, it's silly, but before I became a TQ black belt, I used to feel like a hamster on a wheel at work. TQ helped me and everyone else at DroneZone get control of our lives."

As she recounted her rise from Emerging Techie to Techspert, I thought back fondly to our chance encounter outside the Camelback Café.

As the podcast continued, she became more and more excited, explaining all about the TQAT, tech types, and zip tips. And I realized something: TQ isn't new. It's always been there, helping a select few, like Edison, Curie, and the Wrights, who were able to unravel its mystery and harness its potential.

But now, with the help of the TQAT and black belts like Claire, TQ was coming into sharp focus for the rest of the world. It was emerging day by day as a majestic, powerful, and rock-solid bridge to the **Future of Work**.

ACKNOWLEDGEMENTS

Special thanks to all the fantastic people who contributed their time, effort, ideas, and energy to this book. I am grateful. Life is short. I am so glad that I've had the chance to collaborate with such fine colleagues.

Greg Watts (Editor)
Greisy Flores
Donna Dvorak
Elena Song
Jeff Burress
Tim Burress
Liza Rivera
Vicki Halsey
Will Mahon
Pamela Orner
Drew Foster
Barry Viviano
Jill Fuller
Cynthia Farquhar
Bill Kirwin
Jim Irvine
Pat Larkin

Donna Dvorak
Matt Koch
Lucinda Ehlen
Annah Litzenberger
Ginny Zub
Doug Shupinski
Sharifa Austin
Adrian Magirl
Rachel Osteen (Editor)
Renee Hosonitz
Jo Walsh
John Ireland
Ric Torres

INDEX

ABOUT THE AUTHOR

Mike Song is an award-winning tech blogger and author of the bestselling Hamster Revolution book series. Mike is widely regarded as one of the best virtual presenters in the world. Mike has helped millions get more done via dynamic interviews with CNN, NPR, and FOX. Mike and his team created the ground-breaking TQ Assessment Tool (TQAT^{SM}), which sorts professionals into four distinct tech types. He has conducted over 100,000 workplace surveys while providing training to over 20% of the Global 1000. Contact Mike at info@getcontrol.net or @getmoredone on Twitter.

THE HAMSTER BOOK SERIES

1. **The Hamster Revolution:** Manage Your Email Before It Manages You

2. **The Hamster Revolution for Meetings:** How to Meet Less and Get More Done

3. **Zip Tips!** The Fastest Way to Get More Done

4. **The Hamster Revolution for TQ:** How to Thrive in the Post-Covid, Virtual World of Work

TQ AT YOUR ORGANIZATION

Are you interested in taking the TQAT? You can! Visit www.getcontrol.net or email us at tq@getcontrol.net. Our TQ program is part of *Get Control!* University; a virtual, tech-driven time management training center.

We've developed state-of-the-art e-learning, video, keynote, and webinars that boost TQ and performance. We focus on these crucial areas:

- Virtual Meeting, Presentation, Sales, and Leadership Skills
- Tech-Driven Time Management Best Practices
- Digital Office Organization via Microsoft 365 and Google
- TQAT Assessment and training.

If you would like a training brochure or demo, visit www.getcontrol.net or email us at info@getcontrol.net.

ENDNOTES

[i] Jaccques Bughin et al., Skill Shift, Automation and the Future of the Workforce, Mckinsey Global Institute, May 2018.

[ii] Frankiewicz, [2020, May 6]. Digital Transformation Is About Talent, Not Technology

https://hbr.org/2020/05/digital-transformation-is-about-talent-not-technology

[iii] Thomas, [2015, April 22]. Time Management Training Doesn't Work

https://hbr.org/2015/04/time-management-training-doesnt-work

[iv] Vogels, [2019, September 9]. Millennials stand out for their technology use, but older generations also embrace digital life https://www.pewresearch.org/fact-tank/2019/09/09/us-generations-technology-use/

[v] Fernandez, [2014, July 7]. How the Digital Skills Gap bleeds $1.3 Trillion a Year From US Businesses, https://www.entrepreneur.com/article/235366

[vi] M. Song, B. Kirwin, *Get Control of Technology Research*, 2019, GetControl.net, n=120,311

[vii] Accengage {2018}, 2018 Push Notification & In-App Message Benchmark Study https://www.accengage.com/white-paper-request-confirmation/

[viii] Iqbal & Horvitz, [2007]. Disruption and Recovery of Computing Tasks: Field Study, Analysis, and Directions, Univ. of Illinois & Microsoft Research

[ix] Perkin {2017, September 21} Systems Thinking in Modern Business, Business Agility,https://agilebusinessmanifesto.com/agilebusiness/systems-thinking-modern-business/